THE BEST OF
BROCHURE DESIGN 6

ROCKPORT

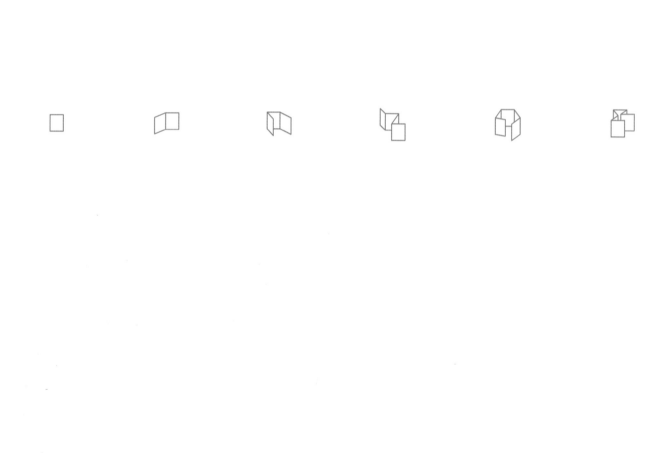

THE BEST OF
BROCHURE DESIGN 6

GLOUCESTER MASSACHUSETTS

ROCKPORT
PUBLISHERS

First published in the United States of America by
Rockport Publishers, Inc.
33 Commercial Street
Gloucester, Massachusetts 01930-5089
Telephone: (978) 282-9590
Facsimile: (978) 283-2742
www.rockpub.com

ISBN 1-56496-739-5

10 9 8 7 6 5 4 3 2 1

Design: Stoltze Design

Printed in China.

TECNICI CON UNA FORTE
IDENTITÀ, FUNZIONALI, CREATIVI,
UNICI E RARI PER MIGLIORARE
LA QUALITÀ DELLA VITA. IDEE DI
PRODOTTO, MA ANCHE DI
ORGANIZZAZIONE E DI SERVIZI
PER RISPONDERE SEMPRE
MEGLIO ALLE DOMANDE DEL
NUOVO MILLENNIO
ARE BORN FROM INTUITION,
FROM THE RESEARCH AND
EXPERIENCE GAINED FROM
TECHNOLOGY. TOGETHER WITH
CLIENTS, TRENDS AND MARKET
DEMANDS. AIM: TO CREATE
TECHNO FABRICS WITH A
STRONG IDENTITY, FUNCTIONAL,
CREATIVE AND UNIQUE TO
IMPROVE THE QUALITY OF LIFE.
PRODUCT IDEAS BUT ALSO
ORGANIZATION AND SERVICES
TO RESPOND INCREASINGLY

DESIGN FIRM › Gregory Thomas Associates
ART DIRECTORS › Gregory Thomas, Alice Flanjak, David La Cava
DESIGNERS › Gregory Thomas, Alice Flanjak, David La Cava
ILLUSTRATOR/PHOTOGRAPHER › In House
COPYWRITERS › David La Cava, Todd Hays
CLIENT › Baskin-Robbins International
TOOLS (SOFTWARE/PLATFORM) › Cut and paste montage; no computer
PRINTING PROCESS › Offset

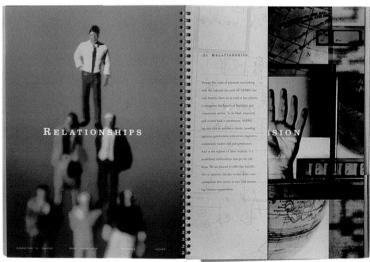

DESIGN FIRM > Base Art Co.
ART DIRECTOR > Terry Alan Rohrbach
DESIGNER > Terry Alan Rohrbach
ILLUSTRATOR/PHOTOGRAPHER > Photonica
COPYWRITER > Hilary Rubin
CLIENT > The SAR Building Group
TOOLS (SOFTWARE/PLATFORM) > QuarkXPress, Photoshop, Macintosh G4
PAPER STOCK > Strobe 100 lb. text; Kaos 100 lb. cover
PRINTING PROCESS > Offset, with foil-stamped emboss

Kulturfreunde

Tuttlingen für Kulturfreunde

Für kulturfreunde ist in Tuttlingen das ganze Jahr über etwas geboten. Musik, Theater und Kabarettabende, aber auch Sportevents wie die DTB-Gala, die große Sportgala des Deutschen Turnerbundes, finden Sie in fast jeder Woche des Jahres.

Beim Honberg Sommer, dem großen Zeltfestival auf dem Honberg, treten jeweils über zwei Wochen im Juli Webstars, aktuelle deutsche Künstler und regionale Acts auf. Freunde von Rock, Pop, Folk, Jazz, Soul und anderen musikalischen Stilrichtungen kommen hier auf ihre Kosten.

Oder darf es ein Comedy, Varieté- oder Kabarettmahnestückchen sein? In der Reihe „Bühne im August" im Stadtteil Möhringen präsentiert die Stadt ausgesuchte kleinkunstveranstaltungen aus den Sparten Kabarett, Chanson, Comedy, Varieté und Musik. Der enge Kontakt zu den auftretenden Künstlern und die tolle Atmosphäre in der Angelhalle machen jede Veranstaltung zu einem unvergesslichen Erlebnis.

Das Honbergfestival mit internationalen Musikern

Stadtfest im Juni

Tuttlingen für Gesellige

In Tuttlingen wird das ganze Jahr über viel gefeiert und gefestet.

Im Februar hat die schwäbisch-alemannische Fasnet Tuttlingen fest im Griff. Spätestens mit dem „Schmotzigä Dunschtig" übernehmen die Narren in der Stadt das Regiment und da gibt es dann vor allem im Stadtteil Möhringen einige Ereignisse, die Sie nicht versäumen sollten.

Das „Fest der freundschaftlichen Begegnung" findet alljährlich im Mai/Juni auf dem Marktplatz statt. Hier vermitteln Menschen aus über 70 Ländern Eindrücke von ihren kulturellen Besonderheiten und gastronomischen Spezialitäten.

Am letzten Juniwochenende hat das Tuttlinger Stadtfest seinen festen Platz. An über 100 Ständen werden Unterhaltung, Information, Speisen und Getränke angeboten. Eine Gastronomiestraße, Straßenkünstler, der Stadtteilmarkt in der Bahnhofstraße und ein buntes Programm auf zahlreichen Bühnen sorgen für eine großartige Atmosphäre auf beiden Seiten der Donau.

Im August können Sie auf der „Tuttlinger Weinstraße" den Urlaub in vollen Zügen genießen. Rund um den Place de Draguignan bieten Ihnen Tuttlinger Wirte ein abwechslungsreiches gastronomisches Angebot. Bei einem attraktiven musikalischen Rahmenprogramm darf es dann auch mal das eine oder andere Viertele mehr sein.

Mittelalterlicher Markt

Weinstraße im August

Gesellige

DESIGN FIRM > revoLUZion - Studio für Design
ART DIRECTOR > Bernd Luz
DESIGNERS > Bernd Luz, Timo Wenda
ILLUSTRATOR/PHOTOGRAPHER > Bernd Luz
COPYWRITER > Sonja Liebsch
CLIENT > Stadt Tuttlingen
TOOLS (SOFTWARE/PLATFORM) > QuarkXPress, Macintosh

DESIGN FIRM › Emery Vincent Design
ART DIRECTOR › Garry Emery
DESIGNER › Emery Vincent Design
CLIENT › Bligh Voller Nield Architects
TOOLS (SOFTWARE / PLATFORM) › QuarkXPress, Illustrator, Photoshop

ANNUAL REPORT

AFTERMARKET
TECHNOLOGY CORP.

DESIGN FIRM > Critt Graham + Associates
ART DIRECTOR > Deborah Pinals
DESIGNER > Kimie Ishii
ILLUSTRATOR > Kimie Ishii
PHOTOGRAPHER > Michael Grecco
COPYWRITER > Mary Ryan
CLIENT > Aftermarket Technology Corp.
TOOLS (SOFTWARE/PLATFORM) > Macintosh
PAPER STOCK > Fox River Coronado, text; Champion Carnival, cover
PRINTING PROCESS > Offset

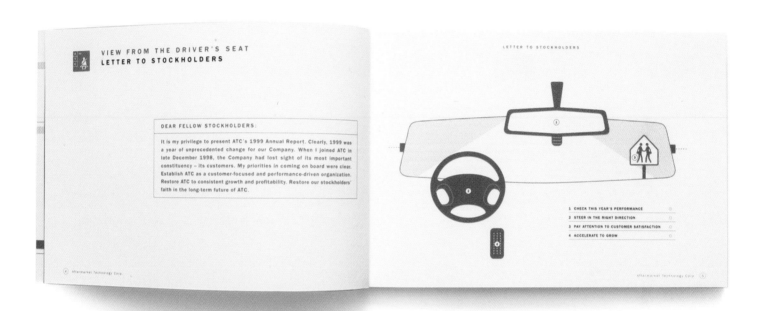

BEUNSTOPPABLE

Compaq is the *NonStop* Internet Company.

That's a pretty bold thing to say, for sure. But it describes, in fact, both how we're working and what we're delivering every day all around the world to help individuals and corporations compete and win in this new, networked world.

The details get technical very quickly. But the essence and excitement are easy to explain. We're pioneering or assembling all the elements needed – from platforms to services – for *NonStop* business performance and anywhere, anytime access to the network. We're helping our customers become, quite literally, unstoppable.

Few can do this.

But any company can describe itself any way it wants to. We'd like to show you how we're doing it. Right now.

UN
STOP
PABLE

DESIGN FIRM › Critt Graham + Associates
ART DIRECTOR › Kai Siang Toh
DESIGNER › Kai Siang Toh
PHOTOGRAPHER › George Lange
COPYWRITER › Chuck Boyer
CLIENT › Compaq Computer Corporation
TOOLS (SOFTWARE/PLATFORM) › Macintosh
PAPER STOCK › Appleton Utopia
PRINTING PROCESS › Offset

how do you handle 100 customer queries an hour, then 1,000,000 an hour?

how do you deploy applications on the Internet quickly?

how do you hook up everything so that it works

how do you win in the Internet economy

with everything else ...all the time?

how do you run e-commerce and e-business NonStop™?

how do you gain access to the Internet from anywhere, anytime?

and how do you find the coolest stuff to make it all work for you?

24 x 7 x Compaq

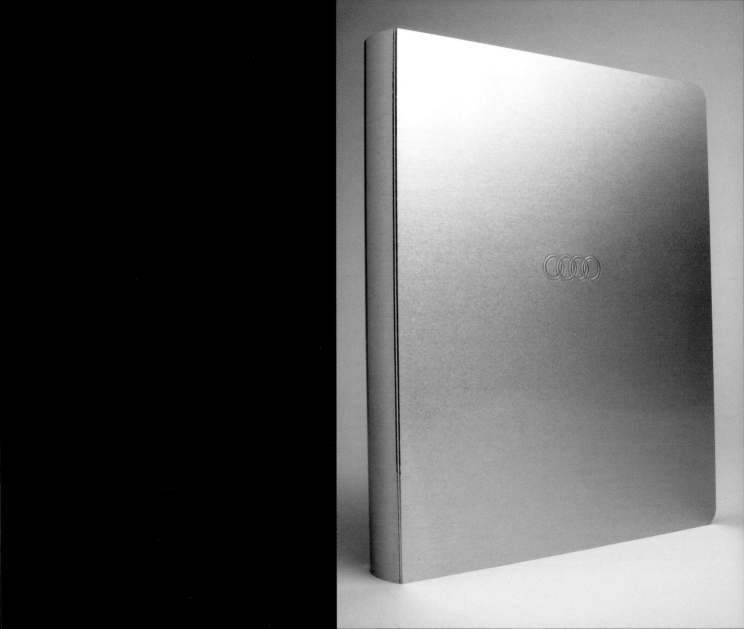

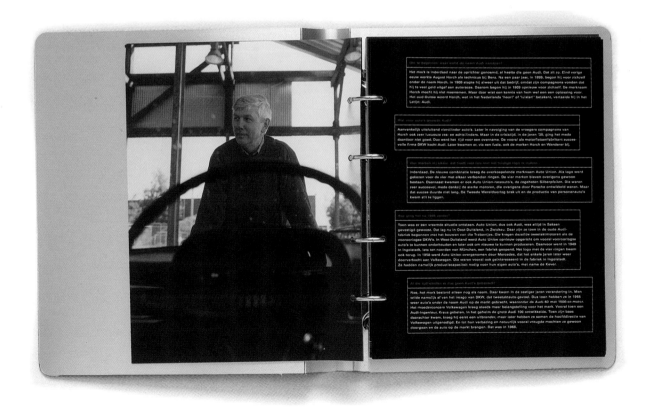

DESIGN FIRM › LA Weekly
ART DIRECTOR › Bill Smith
DESIGNER › Bill Smith
CLIENT › LA Weekly
TOOLS (SOFTWARE/PLATFORM) › QuarkXPress, Photoshop

LA WEEKLY

Simultaneously we sought to provide real alternative thinking and options, whether it was through covering holistic health, visionary human potential movement leaders, or solutions to social conditions proffered by local grassroots activists.

On the cultural front, first off we wanted to be a real writer's paper. Also, we had a vision of creating a home base for the unheard smart voices, the new visions, and the artistic creativity exploding in the community — for instance, we opened the pages to the power of the punk and new wave music movements and put together a remarkable team of movie reviewers.

A big part of the vision was to help forge a real citywide community out of what we found to be a collection of adjacent neighborhoods that scarcely knew about each other. We sought to show readers the richness of who they were, the wealth of remarkable places and people all around the L.A. basin, and the creative and intellectual juices actually surging here outside the entertainment industry. Our vision was extremely democratic — we wanted to be the people's hip paper that celebrated the rebel in everyone. We very much wanted to be a paper that people took personally because it had heart and soul as well as good information.

— Jay Levin, Founding Editor

2

20 YEARS OF *LA WEEKLY*

It's hard to imagine life in Los Angeles without the *LA Weekly*. Since the first edition appeared 20 years and over 1,000 issues ago, there have been millions of words, photos, ads, cartoons and illustrations; thousands of bands, movies, plays and books reviewed; popular and unpopular positions taken, readers moved and offended, lives and a city transformed. For a whole generation, it's always been there, letting people know what's happening, helping to define L.A., telling stories, offering opinions. And, like that first issue, it's still free.

3

LA Weekly's groundbreaking coverage of the conflicts in Central America, environmental issues and the local arts scene generated widespread publicity, won numerous awards and played a significant role in shaping the life of the city.

THE LIST OF L.A.'S FIVE MOST UNDERREPORTED STORIES OF '96 INCLUDED THE PERILS OF THE AEROSPACE INDUSTRY'S WAR ON A PEACE ORGANIZATION, AND THE COUNTY'S AMBIVALENCE TOWARD THE NEEDY.

FACING AIDS

10

magazine called *L.A. Style*, edited by Joie Davidow. This magazine, the result of the fashion boom of the mid-'80s, catered to advertisers and readers who were already familiar with the *Weekly*'s format but wanted a glossy vehicle. During the mid-'80s, *L.A. Style* was one of the fastest-growing magazines in the country and winner of many design awards. In 1988, *L.A. Style* was sold to American Express Publishing.

Throughout the 1980s, *LA Weekly* continued to cover the city — and the nation and the world — from an alternative point of view. Its groundbreaking coverage of the conflicts in Central America, environmental issues and the local arts scene generated widespread publicity, won numerous awards and played a significant role in shaping the life of the city. In-depth articles on politics, on poverty and race, on culture, which could not be found in any other publication, caused elected officials to respond and citizens to become active.

In 1988, as Jay Levin became involved in other

11

SOME EXCEPTIONAL L.A. HEALERS

CONTINUING ITS COVERAGE OF THE BURGEONING HOLISTIC HEALTH MOVEMENT, THE WEEKLY PROFILED FOUR L.A. HEALERS WITH DISTINCTLY DIFFERENT METHODS.

The *Weekly* would cover the offbeat in L.A., not by those pointing a touristic finger and saying, "Oh, isn't this odd?" but by those who lived it.

ON THE EVE OF THE CALIFORNIA NUCLEAR FREEZE INITIATIVE CAMPAIGN, THE WEEKLY PROFILED A LEADER OF THE ANTI-NUCLEAR WAR MOVEMENT AND A SURVIVOR OF HIROSHIMA.

NUCLEAR WAR!! ...THERE GOES MY CAREER!

4

Jay Levin, a journalist who was editor of Flynt Publications' *L.A. Free Press* when it folded in 1978, had a vision of Los Angeles as a disparate group of towns that could be linked together and galvanized by a newspaper like the *Weekly* — one that would inform readers all over the city about what was going on in the arts, politics, movies and music. The *Weekly* would cover the offbeat in L.A., not by those pointing a touristic finger and saying, "Oh, isn't this odd?" but by those who lived it. It would create a sense of community among the myriad local neighborhoods.

After the demise of the *Free Press*, Levin approached local businesses and entertainment figures for their support of a new weekly paper in L.A. Actor-producer Michael Douglas and entrepreneur Pete Kameron were among the original investors in the project and remained on its board of directors for many years.

In November of 1978, with Jay Levin as editor, Joie Davidow as Calendar editor

5

DESIGN FIRM > Melissa Passehl Design
ART DIRECTOR > Melissa Passehl
DESIGNER > Melissa Passehl
PHOTOGRAPHER > Robert Cardin
COPYWRITER > Susan Sharpe
CLIENT > Applied Materials
TOOLS (SOFTWARE/PLATFORM) > Macintosh, QuarkXPress
PAPER STOCK > Starwhite Vicksburg
PRINTING PROCESS > Four-color PMS

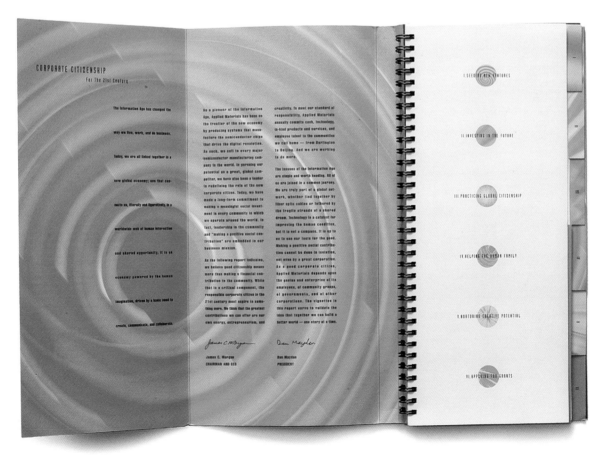

DESIGN FIRM > Country Companies Design Services
ART DIRECTOR > Tracy Griffin Sleeter
DESIGNER > Tracy Griffin Sleeter
PHOTOGRAPHER > Stock Photography
COPYWRITER > Greg Martin
CLIENT > Agency
TOOLS (SOFTWARE/PLATFORM) > Macintosh
PAPER STOCK > Frasier
PRINTING PROCESS > Offset by original Smith printing

The Big Dance

Hyatt Regency San Diego
San Diego, California
June 30 - July 5, 2001

What better way to reward your efforts than a trip the entire family will enjoy - to beautiful San Diego, California? If you've never been there, or haven't been there for awhile, you'll be amazed how much there is to do and see.

San Diego is an excellent place the whole family can enjoy. If you're looking for a wild time, you'll find three of the wildest just minutes away - Sea World, Wild Animal Park and the world-famous San Diego Zoo. Looking to enjoy the weather? Rent some bikes, skates or kayaks and soak up the sunshine on Mission Bay or along any of the city's 70 miles of beach.

If golf is your game, you'll like what San Diego County has to offer. 50 public courses to challenge all levels of golfer. From desert landscapes to country hillsides to

views of the Pacific, San Diego has it all, including Torrey Pines Golf Course - home of the Buick Invitational.

Want something a little more relaxing? Enjoy lunch at one of San Diego's ocean-view restaurants. Go antique shopping, stroll the boutiques or take a quiet walk along the beach at sunset. Finish off the day in Gaslamp Quarter, where you'll find one of the city's liveliest nighttime street scenes.

Of course, what would July 4th be without a picnic and fireworks? Following a picnic with all our Big Dance qualifiers and their families, enjoy a front row seat to fireworks right from the grounds of your hotel - the Hyatt Regency San Diego, located on San Diego Bay.

Fun for everyone – that's what San Diego has to offer. And it's a fitting reward for making it to The Big Dance.

Here's how you do it:

Qualification Criteria

Contest Period:
December 1, 1999 - November 30, 2000

Requirements

Agents: Must be ranked in Top 640, based on Contest Credits. Must have produced at least 48 Contest Units.

Agencies: Must be ranked in Top 64, based on Contest Credits Percent Base. Must have met at least 90 percent of Contest Unit Base.

Experience Factors

Contest Credits vary, based on the length of time a person has served as a Country Companies agent, as shown below. These factors will also impact the agency's Contest Credit totals.

Agent Experience (As of 12-1-1999):
Contest Credits Received

Basic Needs Agents
125% of Contest Credits Earned

0-12 months
120% of Contest Credits Earned

13-24 months
115% of Contest Credits Earned

25-36 months
110% of Contest Credits Earned

37-48 months
105% of Contest Credits Earned

More than 48 months
100% of Contest Credits Earned

The Big Dance.

That's what fans call the NCAA Division I tournament. And whether they say so or not, everyone who loves college basketball wants to make it there. Little else matters. Because regardless of the success a player, coach or team enjoys, they all dream of making it to "the dance."

It's a reward for a year's worth of focus and effort. It's about talent and heart and making sacrifices others did not. It's about doing what it takes to rise above the rest. It's about fulfilling a dream and earning the *National Champion's ring.*

This year, we're introducing our own version of *"The Big Dance."* It, too, will reward focus, heart and sacrifice. It, too, will be about fulfilling dreams.

Are You Ready to Play?

At the end of each NCAA season, 64 teams are invited to 'the dance.' Once the tourney begins, the field quickly narrows. *From 64 to 32, from 32 to the 'Sweet Sixteen,' 'Elite Eight' and 'Final Four.'* The battles end only after the *National Champion* has been crowned.

In our dance, agents and agencies will compete during a yearlong contest. At the conclusion, we will rank all agents and agencies based on their performance. The **Top 640 agents and 64 agencies** meeting our contest requirements will earn their invitation to **The Big Dance** and participate in our **National Tournament**. We'll host two very special **All Star trips** for all agents and managers meeting our midyear qualification requirements, too.

Here's Your Letter

We've attached your letter to this book, to help serve as a reminder of your goals during this contest. Each step of the way, from **All Star** to **The Big Dance** and beyond, we'll award a special pin to all that qualify. It's a mark of distinction shared by a select few...those who pay the price to be among the best.

Here's Your Playbook

This book contains everything you need to know about **The Big Dance.** How the contest works. How to earn your invitation. And most importantly, all the great prizes you can win along the way if you've got what it takes to make it to the dance. *Interested?* Take a look inside to learn more.

DESIGN FIRM > Hand Made Group
ART DIRECTORS > Alessandro Esteri, Giona Maisrelli
DESIGNERS > Alessandro Esteri, Giona Maisrelli
ILLUSTRATOR/PHOTOGRAPHER > Alessandro Esteri
COPYWRITER > Verdiana Maggiorelli
CLIENT > Microtex S.P.A.
TOOLS (SOFTWARE/PLATFORM) > Apple, QuarkXPress, Freehand, Photoshop
PAPER STOCK > Zanders
PRINTING PROCESS > Printed in Pantone

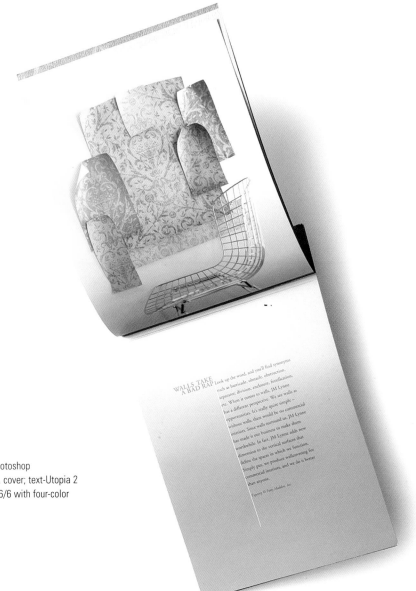

DESIGN FIRM › Grant Design Collaborative
ILLUSTRATOR/PHOTOGRAPHER › Maria Robledo
CLIENT › JM Lynne Co., Inc.
TOOLS (SOFTWARE/PLATFORM) › Macintosh, QuarkXPress, Photoshop
PAPER STOCK › Cover—Mohawk Tomohawk New Smoke 65 lb. cover; text-Utopia 2
PRINTING PROCESS › Cover—foil Stamp with two PMS; text—6/6 with four-color and two PMS

a conscium business

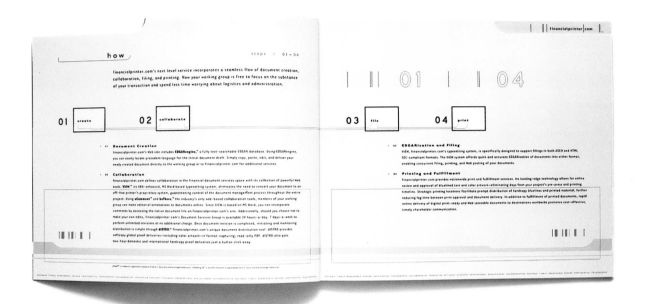

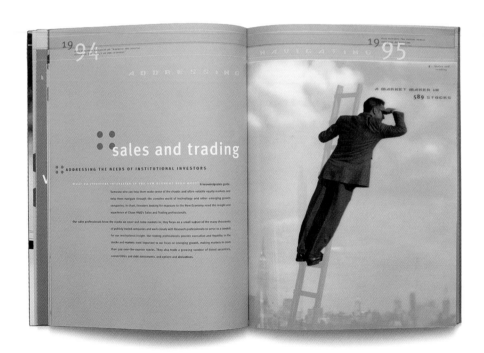

DESIGN FIRM > Michael Patrick Partners
ART DIRECTOR > Dan O'Brien
DESIGNER > Connie Hwang
ILLUSTRATOR/PHOTOGRAPHER > Various
COPYWRITER > Tim Peters
CLIENT > Chase H & Q
PAPER STOCK > Cornado, 100 lb. text, Fox River Company
PRINTER > Graphics Center

DESIGN FIRM > Michael Courtney Design
ART DIRECTORS > Mike Courtney, Scott Souchok
DESIGNERS > Mike Courtney, Scott Souchok
PHOTOGRAPHER > Stock, Kevin Latona
COPYWRITER > The Frause Group
CLIENT > Vulcan Northwest
TOOLS (SOFTWARE/PLATFORM) > Freehand, Photoshop
PAPER STOCK > Potlatch McCoy
PRINTING PROCESS > Four-color offset

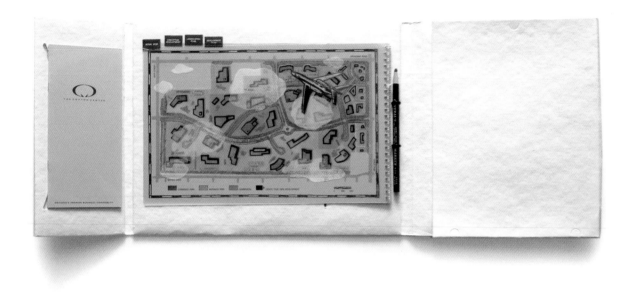

The Cotton Center is 280 acres of extraordinary business opportunity.

Strategically located less than five minutes from Phoenix Sky Harbor International Airport, The Cotton Center provides incomparable access to the entire Phoenix metropolitan area.

Because The Cotton Center is in the center of the region's freeway system, more than 95% of the population of America's sixth largest city lives within 40 minutes of the heart of The Cotton Center.

The affluent and fast-growing communities of Scottsdale, Tempe, Ahwatukee, Chandler, Gilbert and Mesa are within 20 minutes of The Cotton Center.

Arizona State University, with its renowned undergraduate and graduate schools, research facilities, business incubator programs and think-tanks is only 25 blocks away. 19 additional institutions of higher learning are within 20 minutes.

This is not your typical commercial real estate. This is the very definition of a premier business community.

DESIGN FIRM > After Hours Creative
ART DIRECTOR > After Hours Creative
DESIGNER > After Hours Creative
ILLUSTRATOR > Rick Allen
COPYWRITER > After Hours Creative
CLIENT > Cotton Center
TOOLS (SOFTWARE/PLATFORM) > Macintosh G4, Adobe Illustrator

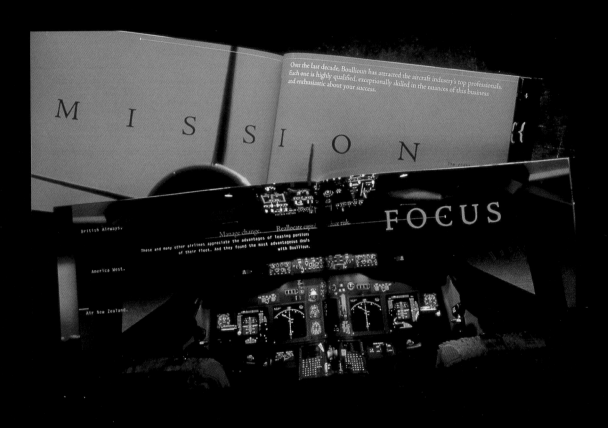

DESIGN FIRM › Hornall Anderson Design Works, Inc.
ART DIRECTORS › Jack Anderson, Katha Dalton
DESIGNERS › Katha Dalton, Ryan Wilderson, Belinda Bowling
PHOTOGRAPHERS › Boeing, West Stock, Tony Stone, Alan Abramowitz
COPYWRITER › John Koval
CLIENT › Boullioun Aviation Services
TOOLS (SOFTWARE/PLATFORM) › QuarkXPress
PAPER STOCK › McCoy, Strathmore

DESIGN FIRM > Cox Design
ART DIRECTOR > Randy Cox
DESIGNER > Randy Cox
COPYWRITER > Mike Furnary
CLIENT > San Jose Mercury News
TOOLS (SOFTWARE/PLATFORM) > Photoshop, QuarkXPress, Macintosh
PAPER STOCK > French
PRINTING PROCESS > Offset

DESIGN FIRM > Hand Made Group
ART DIRECTOR > Alessandro Esteri, Giona Maisrelli
DESIGNER > Alessandro Esteri, Giona Maisrelli
ILLUSTRATOR/PHOTOGRAPHER > Alessandro Esteri
COPYWRITER > Verdiana Maggiorelli
CLIENT > Tessile Fiorentina
TOOLS (SOFTWARE/PLATFORM) > QuarkXpress, Photoshop
PAPER STOCK > Zanders
PRINTING PROCESS > Printed in Pantone

DESIGN FIRM > Gee + Chung Design
ART DIRECTOR > Earl Gee
DESIGNERS > Earl Gee, Qui Tong
PHOTOGRAPHER > Stock
COPYWRITERS > Tracy Harvey, Susan Berman
CLIENT > Netigy Corporation
TOOLS (SOFTWARE/PLATFORM) > QuarkXPress, Adobe Illustrator, Photoshop
PAPER STOCK > Springhill SBS C25 24 pt., Appleton Utopia, 65 lb. cover
PRINTING PROCESS > Offset lithography, die-cut cover

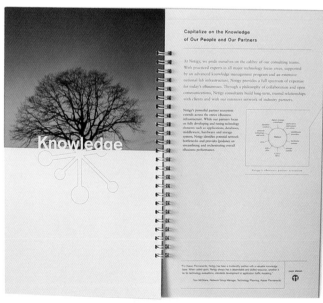

DESIGN FIRM > The Bonsey Design Partnership
ART DIRECTOR > Chris Lee
DESIGNER > Damien Thomasz
PHOTOGRAPHERS > Andrew Hun, Alex Ow
COPYWRITER > Jane Cotter
CLIENT > Transtel Engineering
TOOLS (SOFTWARE/PLATFORM) > Macintosh, Freehand,
Photoshop
PAPER STOCK > Matt art card
PRINTING PROCESS > Five-color plus one special

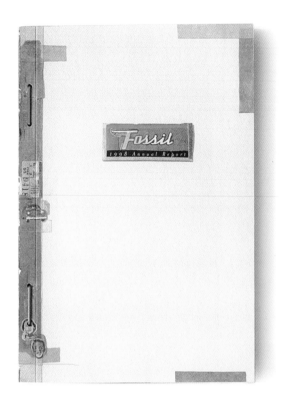

DESIGN FIRM > Fossil
ART DIRECTORS > Tim Hale, Stephen Zhang
DESIGNER > Stephen Zhang
ILLUSTRATORS > Ellen Tanner, Paula Wallace, John Vineyard, Jennifer Burk, Andrea Haynes
PHOTOGRAPHER > Dave McCormack
CLIENT > Fossil
TOOLS (SOFTWARE/PLATFORM) > QuarkXPress, Photoshop, Illustrator, Macintosh G3, Power PC
PAPER STOCK > Fox River Protera
PRINTING PROCESS > Four-color offset

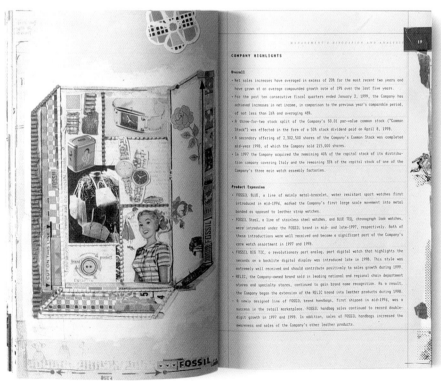

DESIGN FIRM › SamataMason, Inc.
ART DIRECTOR › Greg Samata
DESIGNER › Steve Kull
PHOTOGRAPHERS › Sandro, Marc Norberg, Mark Craig
COPYWRITER › Laurence Pearson
CLIENT › Tupperware Corporation
TOOLS (SSOFTWARE/PLATFORM) › QuarkXPress, Macintosh
PAPER STOCK › Fox River, Coronado Vellum, Fox River Sundance, Canson satin
PRINTING PROCESS › Offset, sheet fed

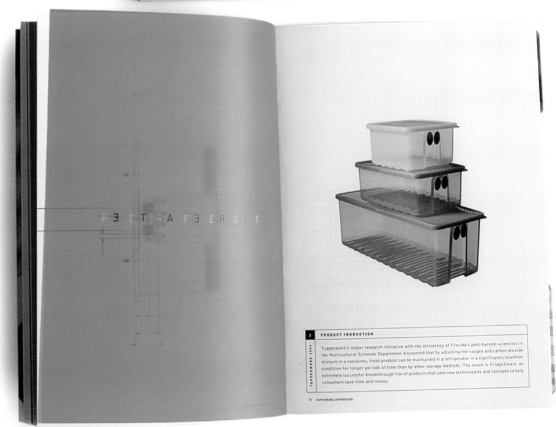

PRODUCT INNOVATION

Tupperware's major research initiative with the University of Florida's post-harvest scientists in the Horticultural Sciences Department discovered that by adjusting the oxygen and carbon dioxide mixture in a container, fresh produce can be maintained in a refrigerator in a significantly healthier condition for longer periods of time than by other storage methods. The result is *FridgeSmart*, an extremely successful breakthrough line of products that uses new technologies and concepts to help consumers save time and money.

DESIGN FIRM > Bloch + Coulter Design Group
ART DIRECTORS > Hollie Hory, Thomas Bloch, Ellie Young Sutt
DESIGNERS > Hollie Hory, Thomas Bloch, Ellie Young Sutt
PHOTOGRAPHER > Jerry Garns
COPYWRITER > Paul Losie
CLIENT > Amwest Insurance Group, Inc.
TOOLS (SOFTWARE/PLATFORM) > Macintosh, QuarkXPress, Photoshop, Illustrator
PAPER STOCK > Editorial: Potlatch Karma 100 lb. text; Flysheet: French Parchtone cream 60 lb. text,
Financial: Beckett embossed enhanced silk 80 lb., text
PRINTING PROCESS > All but cover sheet fed, hand bound with Acco fastener

DESIGN FIRM > Cross Colours Ink
ART DIRECTOR > Janice Beddington
DESIGNER > Janice Beddington
ILLUSTRATOR/PHOTOGRAPHER > David Pastoll
CLIENT > Nando's Chickenland
TOOLS (SOFTWARE/PLATFORM) > Macintosh, Freehand, Photoshop
PRINTING PROCESS > Lithography

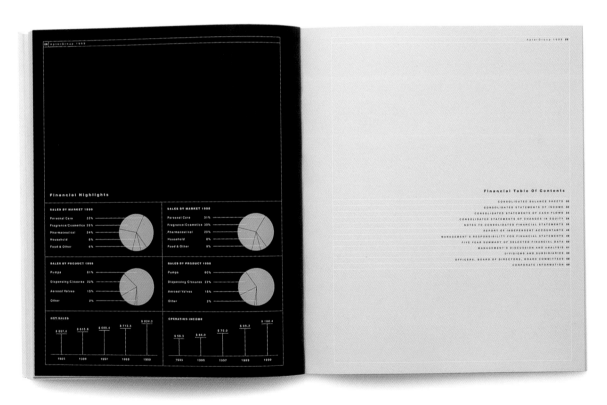

DESIGN FIRM › SamataMason, Inc.

ART DIRECTORS › Pat & Greg Samata

DESIGNER › Kevin Krueger

PHOTOGRAPHER › Sandro

CLIENT › Aptar Group

TOOLS (SOFTWARE/PLATFORM) › QuarkXPress, Macintosh

PAPER STOCK › Appleton—coated Utopia one, dull; Monadnock Aastrolite vellum

PRINTING PROCESS › Offset, sheet fed

DESIGN FIRM › Edelman Public Relations Worldwide

ART DIRECTOR › Mary Ackerly

DESIGNERS › Rosanne Kang, Lana Le

PHOTOGRAPHERS › Josef Astor, Whitney Cox, Doug Levere, Peter Loppacher, William Vasquez

COPYWRITER › Various

CLIENT › Barnes and Noble

TOOLS (SOFTWARE/PLATFORM) › QuarkXpress, Adobe Illustrator, Macintosh

PAPER STOCK › Mohawk 50/10

PRINTING PROCESS › Offset lithography

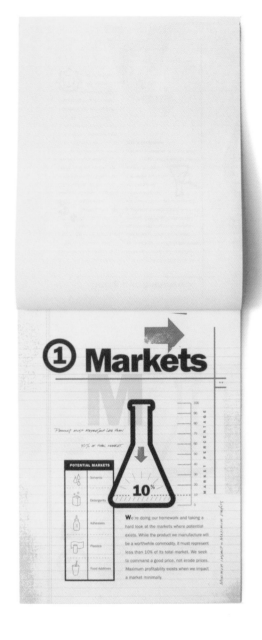

DESIGN FIRM > Greteman Group
ART DIRECTORS > Sonia Greteman, James Strange
DESIGNER > James Strange
PHOTOGRAPHER > Steve Rasmussen
COPYWRITERS > Deanna Harms, Raleigh Drennon
CLIENT > High Plains
TOOLS (SOFTWARE/PLATFORM) > Freehand
PAPER STOCK > Productolith

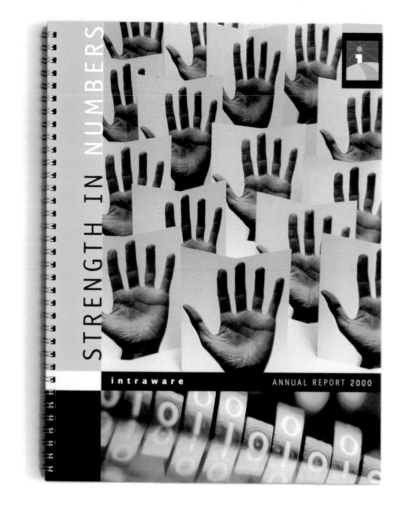

DESIGN FIRM › Intraware, Inc. (Creative Services Group)
ART DIRECTOR › Rudolph O'Meara
DESIGNER › Rudolph O'Meara
ILLUSTRATOR/PHOTOGRAPHER › Stock
COPYWRITERS › Jon Rant, Thea Gray
CLIENT › Intraware, Inc.
TOOLS (SOFTWARE/PLATFORM) › QuarkXPress, Adobe Photoshop, Illustrator
PAPER STOCK › 80 lb. cool white Mohawk, 27 lb. yellow chromatica

One of the reasons that Intraware's customer base grew exponentially over the course of the last year was because of our success in increasing the products and vendors available through our online procurement services. At the close of the fiscal year we sold and supported over 1,500 software and courseware product lines available from more than 60 vendor partners. The software partners included such key FY2000 additions as Hewlett-Packard, Novell, Computer Associates, Vignette, and BEA. Information vendors such as Gartner, Aberdeen Group, Books24x7.com, and Business Week Online, as well as training courseware providers SmartForce and Paragon, have also become Intraware partners in the past fiscal year.

PARTNERSHIPS

We have also increased the number of companies licensing our software management services for use by their own customers. New partners such as PeopleSoft, Commerce One, E.piphany, and Interwoven are now able to reduce costs and offer their customers better service through software update notifications and online access to updates and release archives. The more partners we add, the more the market becomes aware of Intraware's technological expertise—generating the critical mass necessary to strengthen our position as the leading IT e-marketplace. Matchmaker, market maker; with Intraware in the middle, the IT puzzle becomes far less complicated for enterprise users and vendors alike.

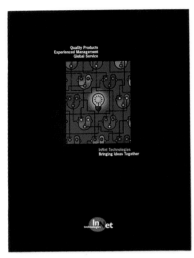

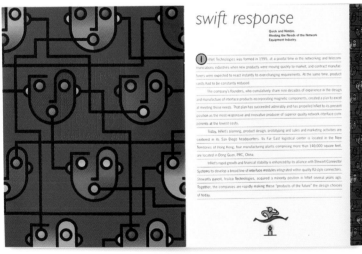

swift response

Quick and Nimble.
Meeting the Needs of the Network
Equipment Industry.

InNet Technologies was formed in 1995, at a pivotal time in the networking and telecommunications industries when new products were moving quickly to market, and contract manufacturers were expected to react instantly to ever-changing requirements. At the same time, product costs had to be constantly reduced.

The company's founders, who cumulatively share nine decades of experience in the design and manufacture of interface products incorporating magnetic components, created a plan to excel at meeting those needs. That plan has succeeded admirably and has propelled InNet to its present position as the most responsive and innovative producer of superior quality network interface components at the lowest costs.

Today, InNet's planning, product design, prototyping and sales and marketing activities are centered in its San Diego headquarters. Its Far East logistical center is located in the New Territories of Hong Kong. Four manufacturing plants comprising more than 140,000 square feet, are located in Dong Guan, PRC, China.

InNet's rapid growth and financial stability is enhanced by its alliance with Stewart Connector Systems to develop a broad line of interface modules integrated within quality RJ-style connectors. Stewart's parent, Insilco Technologies, acquired a minority position in InNet several years ago. Together, the companies are rapidly making these "products of the future" the design choices of today.

DESIGN FIRM › Lorenz Advertising
ART DIRECTOR › Arne Ratermanis
DESIGNER › Arne Ratermanis
ILLUSTRATORS/PHOTOGRAPHERS › Arne Ratermanis, Michael Balderas
COPYWRITER › Carm Greco
CLIENT › InNet Technologies
TOOLS (SOFTWARE/PLATFORM) › QuarkXPress, Illustrator, Macintosh
PAPER STOCK › Potlatch McCoy Gloss
PRINTING PROCESS › Four-color litho with dull and gloss varnish; embossed cover

CONNOISSEUR

PRODUCT **BROCHURES**

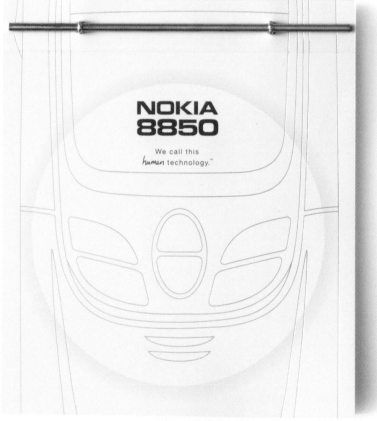

DESIGN FIRM > 141 Singapore Pte Ltd.
ART DIRECTOR > Doris Hiw
DESIGNER > Doris Hiw
ILLUSTRATOR/PHOTOGRAPHER > David Allan Brandt
COPYWRITER > Kok Chin Yin
CLIENT > Nokia Pte Ltd.
PAPER STOCK > 250 gsm Eagle Silohuette premium matt, 155 gsm GSK transparent natural
PRINTING PROCESS > Two-sided, 6c x 7c solid varnish, 1c x 0c tracing, matt silver stamping

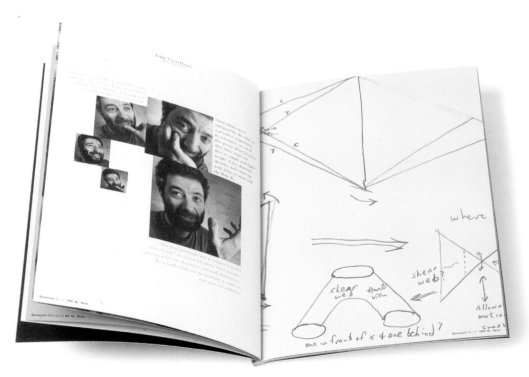

DESIGN FIRM › Douglas Joseph Partners

ART DIRECTORS › Scott Lambert, Doug Joseph

DESIGNER › Scott Lambert

ILLUSTRATORS › Juliette Borda, Eddie Guy

PHOTOGRAPHERS › Dave Teel, Jeff Zaruba, Rick Chou, Eric Tucker, Scott Lambert, Diana Koenigsberg

COPYWRITER › Delphine Hirasuna

CLIENT › Fraser Papers

TOOLS (SOFTWARE/PLATFORM) › QuarkXPress on Macintosh

PAPER STOCK › Fraser genesis, synergy, passport

Uphill and downhill
riding are separate experiences.

Uphill you can have discussions,
think about things.

Downhill is a real "be here now"
experience; it clears your brain out.

If you don't, you crash. I love that feeling
of swooping through things, leaning into the
corners, getting into the groove.

Genesis Marigold 80 lb. Text

Genesis Birch 100 lb. Text

Genesis Birch 100 lb. Text

Genesis Birch 100 lb. Text

Genesis Birch 100 lb. Text

DESIGN FIRM › Emery Vincent Design
ART DIRECTOR › Garry Emery
DESIGNER › Emery Vincent Design
CLIENT › Maxton Fox
TOOLS (SOFTWARE/PLATFORM) › QuarkXPress, Illustrator, Photoshop

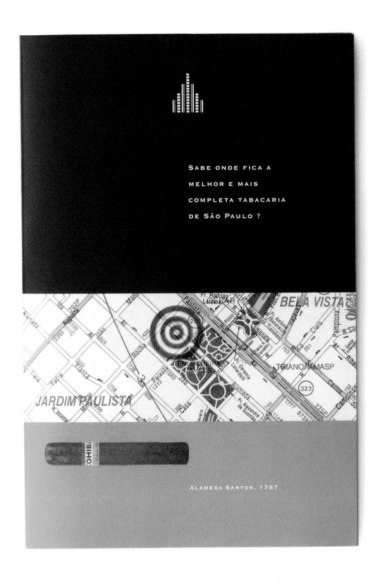

DESIGN FIRM > José J. Dias da S. Junior
ART DIRECTOR > José J. Dias da S. Junior
DESIGNER > José J. Dias da S. Junior
CLIENT > The Cigar Place
TOOLS (SOFTWARE/PLATFORM) > Photoshop, Corel Draw, Page Maker for PC
PAPER STOCK > Unpolished couche

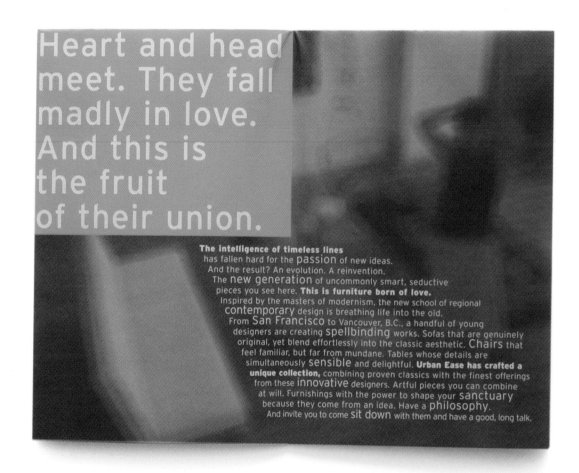

Heart and head meet. They fall madly in love. And this is the fruit of their union.

The intelligence of timeless lines has fallen hard for the passion of new ideas. And the result? An evolution. A reinvention. The new generation of uncommonly smart, seductive pieces you see here. **This is furniture born of love.** Inspired by the masters of modernism, the new school of regional contemporary design is breathing life into the old. From San Francisco to Vancouver, B.C., a handful of young designers are creating spellbinding works. Sofas that are genuinely original, yet blend effortlessly into the classic aesthetic. Chairs that feel familiar, but far from mundane. Tables whose details are simultaneously sensible and delightful. **Urban Ease has crafted a unique collection,** combining proven classics with the finest offerings from these innovative designers. Artful pieces you can combine at will. Furnishings with the power to shape your sanctuary because they come from an idea. Have a philosophy. And invite you to come sit down with them and have a good, long talk.

DESIGN FIRM › Giorgio Davanzo Design
ART DIRECTOR › Giorgio Davanzo
DESIGNER › Giorgio Davanzo
ILLUSTRATOR/PHOTOGRAPHER › Various
COPYWRITER › Mary LaCoste
CLIENT › Urban Ease
TOOLS (SOFTWARE/PLATFORM) › QuarkXPress 4.1, Photoshop 5.5, Illustrator 8.0 for Macintosh
PAPER STOCK › Hammermill via colors Sunflower
PRINTING PROCESS › Offset, two PMS colors

and does it work...?

systematic reflections on a safe future

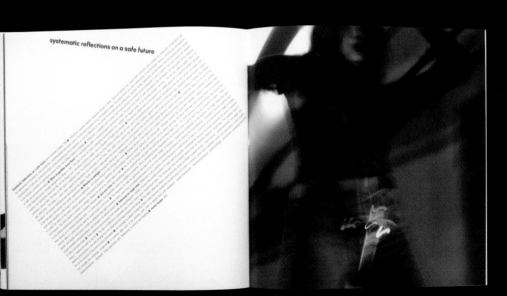

DESIGN FIRM > Emery Vincent Design
ART DIRECTOR > Garry Emery
DESIGNER > Emery Vincent Design Team
CLIENT > Susan Cohn (Jeweller)
TOOLS (SOFTWARE/PLATFORM) > QuarkXPress, Illustrator, Photoshop

do create

DESIGN FIRM › Kesselskramer
ART DIRECTOR › Erik Kessels
DESIGNER › Karen Heuter
ILLUSTRATORS/PHOTOGRAPHERS › Stang, Bianca Pilet
COPYWRITER › David Bell
CLIENT › Do
TOOLS (SOFTWARE/PLATFORM) › QuarkXPress, Apple Macintosh
PAPER STOCK/PRINTING PROCESS › Cyclus print
PRINTING PROCESS › Offset, sheet

DESIGN FIRM > Zappata Diseñadores S.C.
ART DIRECTOR > Ibo Angulo
DESIGNER > Ibo Angulo
PHOTOGRAPHER > Ricardo Trabulsi
CLIENT > Laura Lavalle
TOOLS (SOFTWARE/PLATFORM) > Photoshop, Freehand
PRINTING PROCESS > Offset

DESIGN FIRM > Zappata Diseñadores S.C.
ART DIRECTOR > Ibo Angulo
DESIGNER > Ibo Angulo
COPYWRITER > © Disney/Pixar
CLIENT > Cupa Chups
TOOLS (SOFTWARE/PLATFORM) > Adobe Illustrator
PRINTING PROCESS > Offset

DESIGN FIRM › Damion Hickman Design

ART DIRECTOR › Damion Hickman

DESIGNER › Damion Hickman

ILLUSTRATOR/PHOTOGRAPHER › Greg Nesler

COPYWRITER › David Turner

CLIENT › Turner Bicycles

TOOLS (SOFTWARE/PLATFORM) › Illustrator

DESIGN FIRM › R & M Associati Grafici
ART DIRECTORS › Fontanella, Di Somma, Cesar
DESIGNERS › Fontanella, Di Somma, Cesar
PHOTOGRAPHER › Franco Gargiulo
CLIENT › Pastificio Liguori
TOOLS (SOFTWARE/PLATFORM) › Adobe Illustrator 8.0
PRINTING PROCESS › Offset

DESIGN FIRM > 141 Singapore Pte Ltd.
ART DIRECTOR > Winnie Lee
DESIGNER > Wnnie Lee
ILLUSTRATORS/PHOTOGRAPHERS > Tomek and Eryk Photography Pty
COPYWRITER > Kok Chin Yin
CLIENT > Nokia Pte Ltd.
PAPER STOCK > Cover—112gsm GSK transparent paper; text—210 gsm Eagle Silhouette matt artcard
PRINTING PROCESS > Cover—3c x 0c; text—5c x 5c, solid matt artcard

DESIGN FIRM > Palmquist Creative
ART DIRECTORS > Kurt Palmquist, Kelly Bellcour
DESIGNERS > Kurt Palmquist, Kelly Bellcour
PHOTOGRAPHERS > Rob Wilke, Denver Bryan
COPYWRITER > Client
CLIENT > Field & Stream
TOOLS (SOFTWARE/PLATFORM) > Adobe Pagemaker, Illustrator, Macintosh
PAPER STOCK/PRINTING PROCESS > Frostbrite, 80 lb. book, white

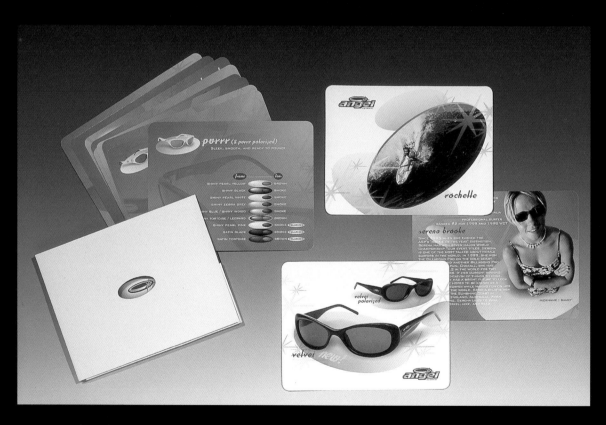

DESIGN FIRM > Alternatives
ART DIRECTOR > Julie Koch-Beinke
DESIGNER > Julie Koch-Beinke
ILLUSTRATOR/PHOTOGRAPHER > Various
CLIENT > Sungold Eyewear
TOOLS (SOFTWARE/PLATFORM) > Illustrator, Macintosh
PAPER STOCK > Metallic pearl white for cover, 100 lb. gloss cover
PRINTING PROCESS > Four-color process

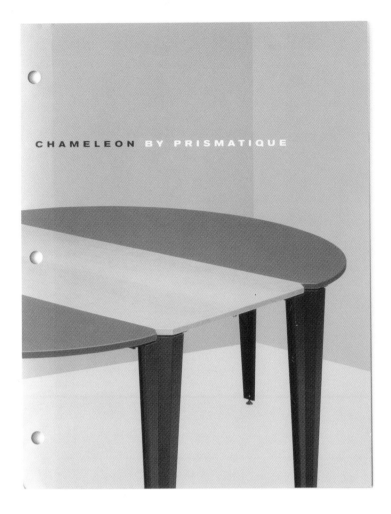

CHAMELEON BY PRISMATIQUE

DESIGN FIRM › Dinnick & Howells
ART DIRECTOR › Jonathan Howells
DESIGNERS › Dwayne Dobson, Tracey Hanson
CLIENT › Prismatique
TOOLS (SOFTWARE/PLATFORM) › Macintosh G3, Illustrator, Photoshop

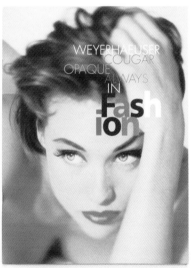

DESIGN FIRM › Sibley Peteet Design
ART DIRECTOR › Don Sibley
DESIGNERS › Don Sibley, Donna Aldridge
PHOTOGRAPHERS › Various
COPYWRITER › Don Sibley
CLIENT › Weyerhaeuser Paper
TOOLS (SOFTWARE/PLATFORM) › QuarkXPress, Macintosh
PAPER STOCK › Weyerhaeuser Cougar opaque

DESIGN FIRM › Creative Conspiracy, Inc.
ART DIRECTOR › Kris Hickcox
DESIGNER › Kris Hickcox
ILLUSTRATOR/PHOTOGRAPHER › Neil Hannum
CLIENT › Screaming Rhino Gift Market
TOOLS (SOFTWARE/PLATFORM) › QuarkXPress, Illustrator, Photoshop
PAPER STOCK/PRINTING PROCESS › Catalog: 80 lb. McCoy–text; 4/4 with bleeds–cover.
Env: 80 lb. Gilbert Voice in Rye

DESIGN FIRM > Arias Associates
ART DIRECTOR > Mauricio Arias
DESIGNER > Mauricio Arias
ILLUSTRATORS/PHOTOGRAPHERS > Mike Halbert, Stefano Massei
COPYWRITER > Pottery Barn
CLIENT > Pottery Barn
TOOLS (SOFTWARE/PLATFORM) > QuarkXPress, Photoshop
PAPER STOCK > Champion Benefit, Mohawk superfine
PRINTING PROCESS > Lithography and letterpress

DESIGN FIRM › Giorgio Rocco Communications
ART DIRECTOR › Giorgio Rocco
DESIGNER › Giorgio Rocco
ILLUSTRATOR/PHOTOGRAPHER › Archives INDA
COPYWRITER › Elisabetta Campo
CLIENT › INDA spa, Italy
TOOLS (SOFTWARE/PLATFORM) › Macintosh, Photoshop, Freehand
PAPER STOCK › Burgo
PRINTING PROCESS › Four-color offset

DESIGN FIRM › Kan & Lau Design Consultants
ART DIRECTORS › Kan Tai-keung, Veronica Cheung, Mak Tsing Kuoh
DESIGNERS › Kan Tai-keung, Veronica Cheung, Mak Tsing Kuoh
COMPUTER ILLUSTRATOR › Ng Cheuk Bong
CLIENT › Rolex (HK) Ltd

DESIGN FIRM > Hand Made Group
ART DIRECTORS > Alessandro Esteri, Giona Maisrelli
DESIGNERS > Alessandro Esteri, Giona Maisrelli
ILLUSTRATOR/PHOTOGRAPHER > Alessandro Esteri
COPYWRITER > Verdiana Maggiorelli
CLIENT > Marco Pierguidi
TOOLS (SOFTWARE/PLATFORM) > QuarkXPress, Photoshop
PAPER STOCK > Garda
PRINTING PROCESS > Four-color

DESIGN FIRM > Oden Marketing and Design
CREATIVE DIRECTOR > Bret Terwilleger
DESIGNER > Michael Guthrie
ILLUSTRATOR > Michael Koelsch
PENCILS > Dean Zachary
COPYWRITER > Henry Ellis
CLIENT > Accent Opaque
PAPER STOCK > Williamson

DESIGN FIRM > Sayles Graphic Design
ART DIRECTOR > John Sayles
DESIGNER > John Sayles
ILLUSTRATOR > John Sayles
COPYWRITER > Wendy Lyons
CLIENT > Sbemco International
TOOLS (SOFTWARE/PLATFORM) > QuarkXPress, Illustrator, Macintosh
PRINTING PROCESS > Offset

DESIGN FIRM › Fossil, Inc.
ART DIRECTORS › Tim Hale, Hans Dorsinville
DESIGNER › Brad Bollinger
PHOTOGRAPHER › Dave McCormick
COPYWRITER › Kathleen Boyes
CLIENT › DKNY Watches
TOOLS (SOFTWARE/PLATFORM) › QuarkXPress 4.0, Photoshop 4.0, Illustrator 8.0, Apple Macintosh G3
PAPER STOCK › Text pages: Bravo matte book, acetate; Cover: Lucence 36 lb.

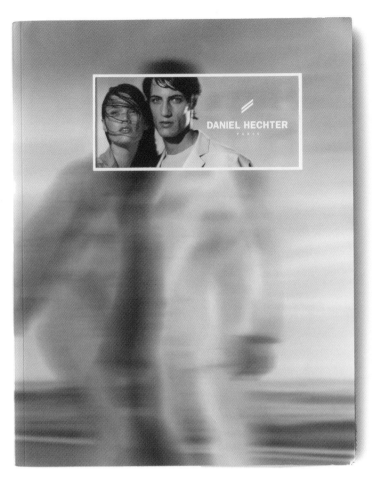

DESIGN FIRM > Hohenhorst Advertising Agency
ART DIRECTOR > Knut Ettling
DESIGNER > Knut Ettling
ILLUSTRATORS/PHOTOGRAPHERS > Michael Williams, Kristian Rahtsen
COPYWRITERS > Birgid Rudolf, Martina Wilde
CLIENT > Daniel Hechter
TOOLS (SOFTWARE/PLATFORM) > QuarkXPress

DESIGN FIRM > Greteman Group
ART DIRECTORS > Sonia Greteman, James Strange
DESIGNERS > James Strange, Craig Tomson
COPYWRITER > Raleigh Drennon
CLIENT > Flexjet
TOOLS (SOFTWARE/PLATFORM) > Freehand
PAPER STOCK > Gloss enamel Carolina C2S

DESIGN FIRM › Gardner Design
ART DIRECTORS › Bill Gardner, Brian Miller, Travis Brown
DESIGNER › Travis Brown
PHOTOGRAPHER › Paul Chauncey
COPYWRITER › John Brown
CLIENT › Excel
TOOLS (SOFTWARE/PLATFORM) › Freehand, Photoshop
PAPER STOCK › Four-color

DESIGN FIRM › Sackett Design Associates

ART DIRECTOR › Mark Sackett

DESIGNERS › James Sakamoto, Wendy Wood, George White

PHOTOGRAPHER › Robert Cardin

COPYWRITER › Bill Bisesto

CLIENT › Spark Online

TOOLS (SOFTWARE/PLATFORM) › Adobe Illustrator, Photoshop, QuarkXPress

PAPER STOCK › Potlatch McCoy silk 80 lb. cover brochures and 120 lb. cover folder

DESIGN FIRM › Pepe Gimeno - Proyecto Gráfico
ART DIRECTOR › Pepe Gimeno
DESIGNER › José P. Gil
CLIENT › International Furniture Fair of Valencia. cDIM
TOOLS (SOFTWARE/PLATFORM) › Freehand 8.0
PRINTING PROCESS › Offset

DESIGN FIRM › Lorenz Advertising
ART DIRECTOR › Glen Miranda
DESIGNER › Glen Miranda
ILLUSTRATORS/PHOTOGRAPHERS › Dan Thoner, various photographers
COPYWRITER › Carm Greco
CLIENT › Enza Zaden North America
TOOLS (SOFTWARE/PLATFORM) › QuarkXPress, Photoshop, Macintosh
PAPER STOCK › Simpson evergreen cord
PRINTING PROCESS › Five-color lithography

DESIGNFIRM › Lee Reedy Creative
ART DIRECTOR › Lee Reedy
DESIGNER › Heather Haworth
ILLUSTRATORS/PHOTOGRAPHERS › Bruce Wolf, Marshal Safron, Michael Peck
COPYWRITER › Carol Parsons
CLIENT › Hunter Douglas
TOOLS (SOFTWARE/PLATFORM) › QuarkXPress
PAPER STOCK › McCoy, laminated and U.V. coated

Contemplate the refined look of raw silk in a series of high performance loop pile patterns.

Select from the 169 imaginative colors of Monterey's universal color system, VIP Traditions.

DESIGN FIRM › Grant Design Collaborative
ILLUSTRATOR/PPHOTOGRAPHER › Geof Kern
CLIENT › Monterey Carpets
TOOLS (SOFTWARE/PLATFORM) › Macintosh, QuarkXPress, Photoshop
PAPER STOCK/PRINTING PROCESS › Cougar opaque 80 lb.
text smooth, 6/6
PRINTING PROCESS › Four-color, PMS, spot varnish

DESIGN FIRM > Burrows
ART DIRECTOR > Reg Malin
DESIGNER > Reg Malin
ILLUSTRATOR/PHOTOGRAPHER > John Cox
COPYWRITER > Joan Dance
CLIENT > Lincoln Mercury
TOOLS (SOFTWARE/PLATFORM) > QuarkXPress, Adobe Illustrator, Photoshop, Apple Power G3
PAPER STOCK > Potlatch McCoy silk
PRINTING PROCESS > Seven-color (three specials), varnish,
spot U.V. printed on a 40-inch Komori press in a single pass in line

DESIGN FIRM > Morla Design
ART DIRECTOR > Jennifer Morla
DESIGNERS > Jennifer Morla, Angela Williams
PHOTOGRAPHER > Jock McDonald
COPYWRITER > Penny Benda
CLIENT > Levi Strauss & Co.
TOOLS (SOFTWARE/PLATFORM) > QuarkXPress
PAPER STOCK > S.D. Warren Company Opus dull 80 lb. cover
PRINTING PROCESS > three-fourths-inch die cut holes on cover

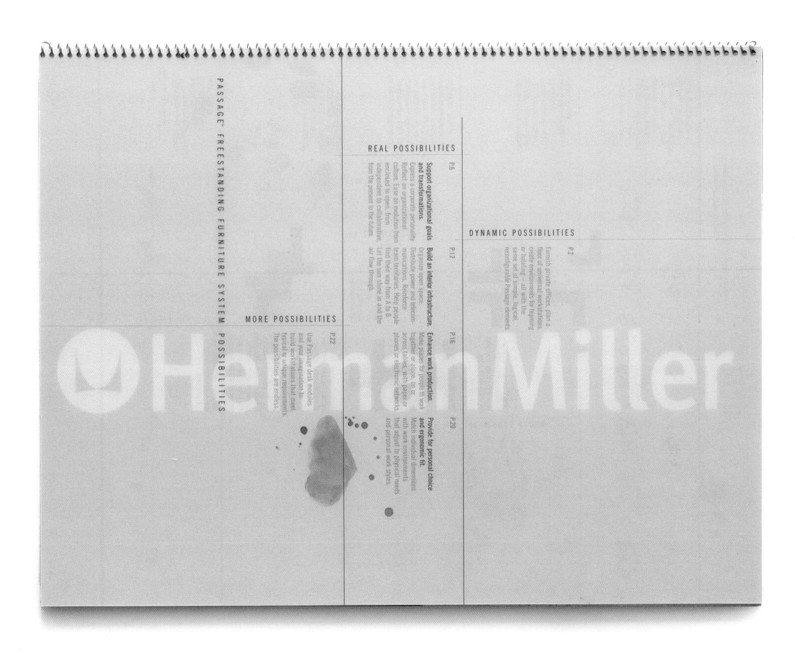

DESIGN FIRM > BBK Studio
ART DIRECTOR > Kevin Budelmann
DESIGNER > Alison Popp
ILLUSTRATORS > Linda Nelson, Mark Schlutt, Kurt Gould
PHOTOGRAPHERS > Nick Merrick, Bob Neumann, Dave Wolters, Susan Carr
COPYWRITER > Deb Wierenga
CLIENT > Herman Miller
TOOLS (SOFTWARE/PLATFORM) > QuarkXPress, Freehand
PAPER STOCK > Nekoosa Solutions and plastic

DESIGN FIRM > Fitch
ART DIRECTORS > Jaimie Alexander, Cindi Pochatek
DESIGNERS > John Jaeckel, Cindi Pochatek, Karyn Kozo, Jim Hanika
ILLUSTRATOR/PHOTOGRAPHER > Stewart Shining
CLIENT > Hush Puppies
PAPER STOCK > Clark Graphics

DESIGN FIRM > Tycoon Graphics
ART DIRECTOR > Tycoon Graphics
DESIGNER > Tycoon Graphics
PHOTOGRAPHER > Shoji Uchida
CLIENT > Abahouse International Co., Ltd.

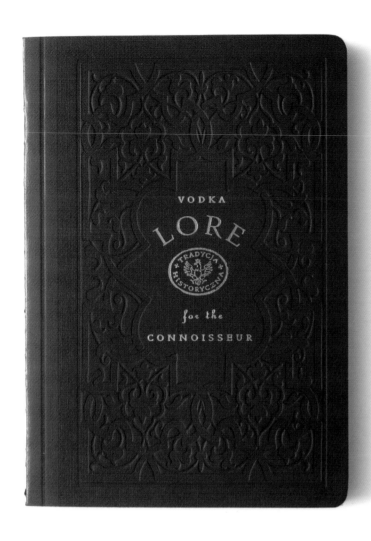

DESIGN FIRM > Clarity Coverdale Fury
ART DIRECTOR > Jac Coverdale
DESIGNER > Jac Coverdale
ILLUSTRATORS > Bill Cook, Peter Sjn, Kate Thomessen, Time Life Books
PHOTOGRAPHER > Raymond Meeks
COPYWRITER > Jerry Fury
CLIENT > Millennium Import Co.
TOOLS (SOFTWARE/PLATFORM) > Illustrator, QuarkXPress, Photoshop, Macintosh
PAPER STOCK > Cover: 130 lb. Curtis back linen; text: 80 lb. Cougar natural smooth
PRINTING PROCESS > Cover: foil stamped, two-colors; text: offset, six-colors, two sides

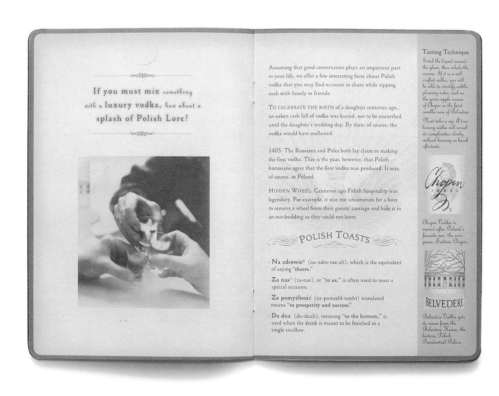

DESIGN FIRM › Sagmeister Inc.
ART DIRECTOR › Stefan Sagmeister
DESIGNER › Stefan Sagmeister
ILLUSTRATOR/PHOTOGRAPHER › Stefan Sagmeister
CLIENT › Anni Kuan Design
TOOLS (SOFTWARE/PLATFORM) › QuarkXPress
PAPER STOCK › Newsprint

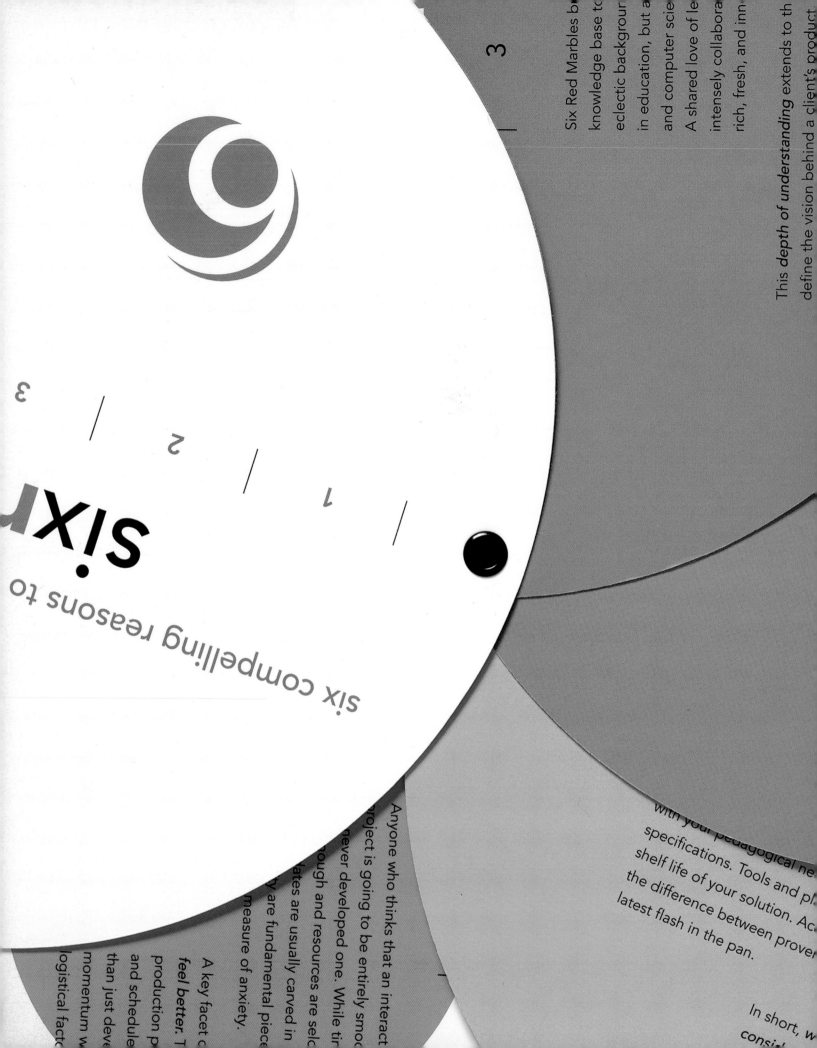

fosters a unique relationship with clients, in
and inspiration at appropriate milestones. T
invariably reflect and exceed the contributi
team members.

6

5

4

e publishing industry can be a scary place these
days; a jungle and an obstacle course rolled into
one. Time-to-market and bottom-line pressures are
more pervasive than ever. Reconciling educational
prerogatives with market realities can seem a
daunting (if not impossible) task.

-hand knowledge of the publishing business has enabled Six
Marbles to emerge as an interactive education leader. We listen
carefully to clients' educational philosophies and state adoption
strategies. We know how to successfully marry print and interactive
media. Our process is designed to accommodate the twists and
turns that publishers face en route to program adoption – from
tight time frames to translation requirements.

5

around.
olutions that square
nd curriculum
ns that maximize the
o experts who know
nologies and the

DESIGN FIRM > Julia Tam Design
ART DIRECTOR > Julia Tam
DESIGNER > Julia Tam
ILLUSTRATORS/PHOTOGRAPHERS > Miscellaneous
COPYWRITER > Dennis Moore
CLIENT > Samjorie Houlihan Lokey
TOOLS (SOFTWARE/PLATFORM) > QuarkXPress, Illustrator
PRINTING PROCESS > Five-color, varnish

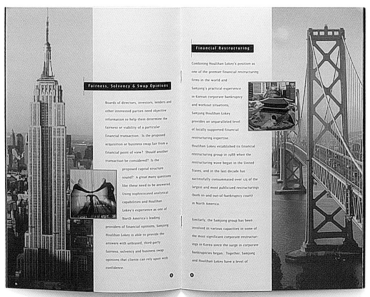

DESIGN FIRM **›** Austin Design
ART DIRECTOR **›** Wendy Austin
DESIGNER **›** Wendy Austin
PHOTOGRAPHER **›** Mark Ferri
CLIENT **›** Mark Ferri Photography
TOOLS (SOFTWARE/PLATFORM) **›** Envelopes, Cromatica, Absinthe, Yellow
PAPER STOCK/PRINTING PROCESS **›** Four-color Heidleberg Press, 100 lb. Potlatch vintage velvet gloss with a dull varnish
PRINTER **›** Arlington Lithograph

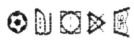

DESIGN FIRM > Kesselskramer

ART DIRECTOR > Erik Kessels

DESIGNER > Erik Kessels

ILLUSTRATOR/PHOTOGRAPHER > Hans Van Der Meer

COPYWRITER > Johan Kramer

CLIENT > Nerol Amsterdam

TOOLS (SOFTWARE/PLATFORM) > QuarkXPress, Apple Macintosh

PAPER STOCK > Semi matt mc

PRINTING PROCESS > Offset

· NAAM: THEO VERGEER · · CLUB: DE GRAAFSCHAP ·

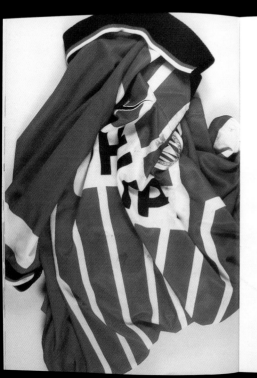

· NAAM: JOHANNA KRUIZE · · CLUB: PSV ·

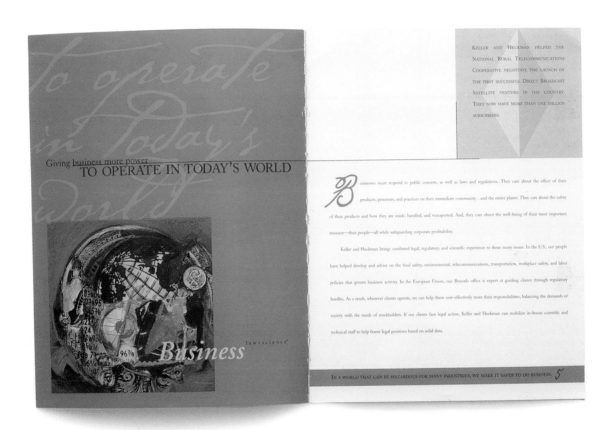

DESIGN FIRM > Jill Tanenbaum Graphic Design & Adv.
ART DIRECTORS > Jill Tanenbaum, Leah Germann
DESIGNERS > Jill Tanenbaum, Leah Germann
COPYWRITER > Jean Podgorsky
CLIENT > Keller & Heckman LLP
TOOLS (SOFTWARE/PLATFORM) > QuarkXPress, Illustrator, Macintosh

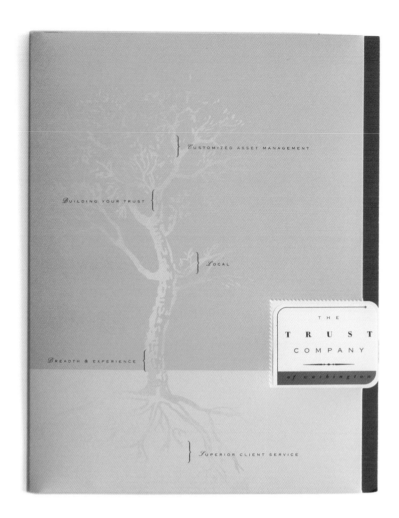

DESIGN FIRM › David Lemley Design
DESIGNERS › David Lemley, Emma Wilson
ILLUSTRATOR/PHOTOGRAPHER › Modified Clip Art
COPYWRITER › Jeff Fraga
CLIENT › The Trust Company of Washington
TOOLS (SOFTWARE/PLATFORM) › Freehand, QuarkXPress, Photoshop, Macintosh OS
PAPER STOCK › Neenah class columns bright white recycled
PRINTING PROCESS › Three PMS double-bumped, offset litho deboss and hand applied tip-in

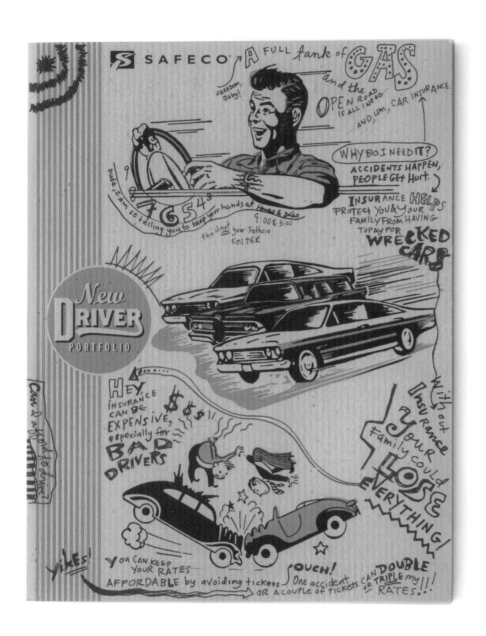

DESIGN FIRM › David Lemley Design
DESIGNERS › David Lemley, Emma Wilson
ILLUSTRATORS/PHOTOGRAPHERS › Modified Clip Art and DLD
COPYWRITER › Derek Dujardin
CLIENT › Safeco
TOOLS (SOFTWARE/PLATFORM) › Freehand, QuarkXPress, Photoshop, Macintosh OS
PAPER STOCK › Neenah classic columns, marigold, indigo
PRINTING PROCESS › Three PMS, offset lithography

DESIGN FIRM > David Lemley Design
DESIGNERS > David Lemley, Emma Wilson
ILLUSTRATORS > David Lemley, Emma Wilson
COPYWRITERS > Rogers & Hammerstein, David Lemley, Emma Wilson
CLIENT > Overlake Press
TOOLS (SOFTWARE/PLATFORM) > Freehand, QuarkXPress, Photoshop, Macintosh OS
PAPER STOCK > French parchtone
PRINTING PROCESS > Four match colors, offset lithography

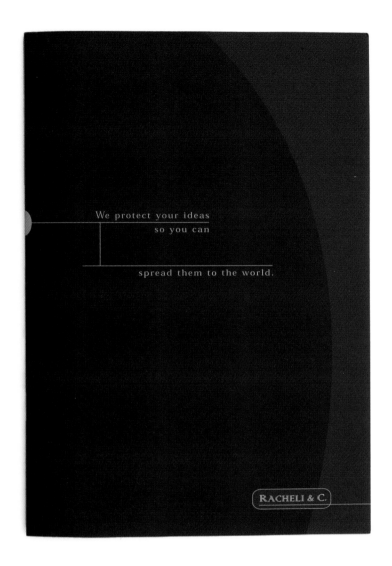

We protect your ideas
so you can

spread them to the world.

RACHELI & C.

DESIGN FIRM > Inox Design, Milan
ART DIRECTOR > Claudio Gavazzi
DESIGNER > Claudio Gavazzi
COPYWRITER > Michela Sartorio
CLIENT > Racheli & Co.
TOOLS (SOFTWARE/PLATFORM) > QuarkXPress
PAPER STOCK > Zanders T2000, two coated papers
PRINTING PROCESS > Three-color offset, opaque varnish, U.V. gloss varnish

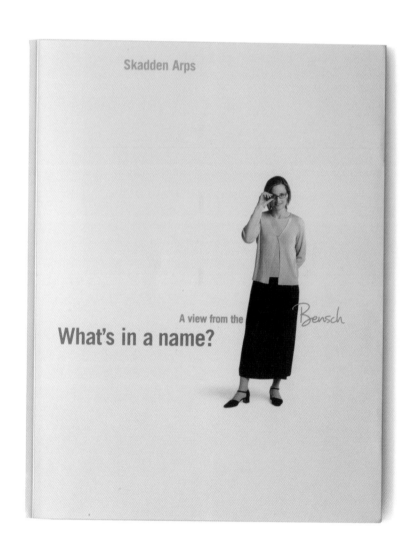

Skadden Arps

A view from the *Bensch*

What's in a name?

DESIGN FIRM › Carbone Smolan Agency
ART DIRECTOR › Justin Peters
DESIGNER › Ken Carbone
PHOTOGRAPHER › Erica Freudenstein
COPYWRITERS › Skadden Arps, Frank Oswald
CLIENT › Skadden Arps
TOOLS (SOFTWARE/PLATFORM) › QuarkXPress 4.1
PAPER STOCK/PRINTING PROCESS › Cover, stock 90 lb. Utopia premium silk white;
text: 115 lb. Utopia premium silk white

Dawn M. Pacifico
Associate, Labor
New York Office

Rutgers University
School of Law, Newark
(J.D., 1998)
Managing Editor, Rutgers
Law Review

Montclair State College
(B.S., 1995)

Law Clerk, Honorable
Richard Newman, New
Jersey Superior Court,
Appellate Division

Dawn of a new age

It's a wired world. And Skadden, Arps is at the
heart of it all. Our clients include a wide range of
tech-savvy firms—from large multinationals
implementing Internet strategies to emerging high-
tech companies in a number of sectors. Our
newest offices in Palo Alto and Northern Virginia
make us one of the few law firms with a presence
in all major U.S. technology markets, including
New York, Boston and LA.

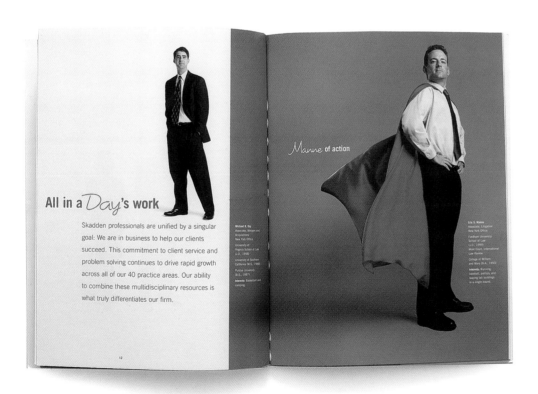

All in a *Day's* work

Skadden professionals are unified by a singular
goal: We are in business to help our clients
succeed. This commitment to client service and
problem solving continues to drive rapid growth
across all of our 40 practice areas. Our ability
to combine these multidisciplinary resources is
what truly differentiates our firm.

Michael R. Day
Associate, Mergers and
Acquisitions
New York Office

University of
Virginia School of Law
(J.D., 1998)

University of Southern
California (M.S., 1990)

Purdue University
(B.S., 1987)

Interests: Basketball and
camping.

Manne of action

Eric S. Manne
Associate, Litigation
New York Office

Fordham University
School of Law
(J.D., 1999)
Moot Court, International
Law Review

College of William
and Mary (B.A., 1993)

Interests: Running,
baseball, politics, and
leaping tall buildings
in a single bound.

At Communications Ventures, few investment opportunities go unseen. One must have a broad view of the industry as well as specific technical expertise to be able to make investment decisions in such a complex area as communications.

We see what others don't.

Our underlying investment philosophy at Communications Ventures is to focus 100% on communications and networking. As a result, we are able to leverage our expertise, better identify exceptional opportunities, and help our portfolio companies achieve long-term success. The partners are willing to "think outside of the box" and look for opportunities that are unique and have great market potential. Once a business plan is received, we are able to react quickly and intuitively.

The partners have the ability to foresee key trends and market opportunities. This in turn has produced some of the most successful start-up companies and the highest returns of any venture firm that invests in the communications industry.

DESIGN FIRM > Gee + Chung Design
ART DIRECTOR > Earl Gee
DESIGNERS > Earl Gee, Fani Chung
PHOTOGRAPHER > Scott Peterson
COPYWRITERS > Kathleen Jensby, Roland Van der Meer
CLIENT > Communications Ventures
TOOLS (SOFTWARE/PLATFORM) > QuarkXPress, Adobe Illustrator, Photoshop
PAPER STOCK > Strathmore Writing bright white wove 110 lb. cover, Potlatch McCoy matte 100 lb. text
PRINTING PROCESS > Offset lithography foil stamping, blind embossing

DESIGN FIRM › Pisarkiewicz Mazur & Co. Inc.
ART DIRECTOR › Mary F. Pisarkiewicz
DESIGNER › Linda Farrer
CLIENT › KLS
TOOLS (SOFTWARE/PLATFORM) › QuarkXPress, Adobe Photoshop
PAPER STOCK › Curtis retrieve black cover, Ikono dull satin text, Chartham steel blue (fly sheets)

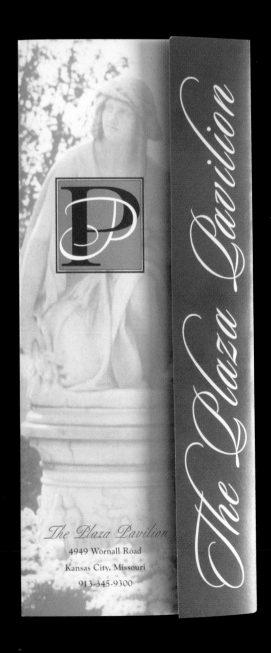

DESIGN FIRM › Tracy Design Communications, Inc.
ART DIRECTOR › Jan Tracy
DESIGNER › Jan Tracy
ILLUSTRATOR/PHOTOGRAPHER › Jan Tracy
COPYWRITER › Katie Van Luchene
CLIENT › The Plaza Pavilion
TOOLS (SOFTWARE/PLATFORM) › QuarkXPress, Photoshop

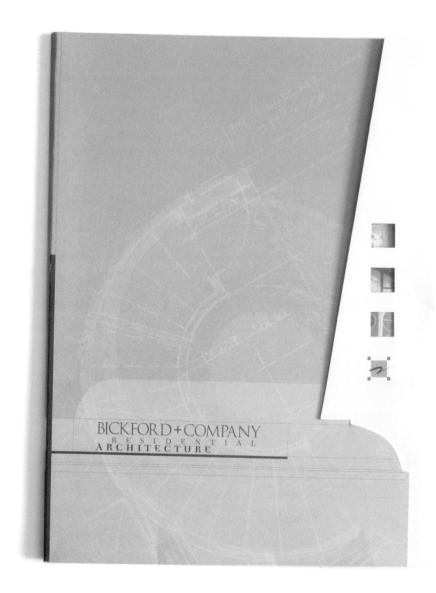

DESIGN FIRM › Tracy Design Communications, Inc.
ART DIRECTOR › Jan Tracy
DESIGNER › Anthony Magliano
ILLUSTRATORS/PHOTOGRAPHERS › Miscellaneous
COPYWRITER › Robin Zaplin
CLIENT › Bickford & Co.
TOOLS (SOFTWARE/PLATFORM) › QuarkXPress, Photoshop

DESIGN FIRM > IE Design
ART DIRECTOR > Marcie Carson
DESIGNER > Marcie Carson
CLIENT > Kern & Wooley LLP
TOOLS (SOFTWARE/PLATFORM) > Macintosh, Illustrator, Photoshop, QuarkXPress
PAPER STOCK/PRINTING PROCESS > Cover: Havana Structeras-Perla; text: Gilbert Oxford Cream
PRINTING PROCESS > Cover: two-color PMJS

DESIGN FIRM ⟩ ie design, Los Angeles
CREATIVE DIRECTOR ⟩ Marcie Carson
DESIGNER ⟩ Marcie Carson
CLIENT ⟩ Good Gracious Events

A boy named Devin had a box of dreams.
It was larger inside than out, it seemed,
for he pulled out a new dream every day,
he dreamed the dream, then tucked it away.
The dreams stayed nice and safe inside,
and no one could take them away if they tried.

DESIGN FIRM › Oden Marketing and Design
CREATIVE DIRECTOR › Bret Terwilleger
DESIGNER › Liz Fonville
ILLUSTRATOR › Bill Berry
COPYWRITERS › Liz Fonville, Sheperd Simmons
CLIENT › Boys and Girls Clubs of Greater Memphis

SOLUTIONS

OSBORN
MALEDON

www.osbornmaledon.com

DESIGN FIRM › After Hours Creative
ART DIRECTOR › After Hours Creative
DESIGNER › After Hours Creative
COPYWRITER › After Hours Creative
CLIENT › Osborn Maledon
TOOLS (SOFTWARE/PLATFORM) › Macintosh G4, Illustrator

COMPLEX

The best lawyers solve complicated problems in ways their clients can understand. • Osborn Maledon attorneys have the judgment, knowledge and experience to bring clarity to complex situations. You receive no nonsense solutions to difficult business issues, from challenging litigation to mergers, acquisitions and public offerings. We know what it takes to get business done. And what it takes to help you achieve your goals. If everything were simple, your choice of a law firm wouldn't matter. When things get complicated, Osborn Maledon offers a clear solution.

CREATIVE

By moving just one glass, arrange the top row to look like the bottom row.

HYDROTHERMAL MASSAGE TUBS IN EVERY ROOM. A FULL RANGE OF
SPA SERVICES. THE FINEST COMFORTS AND AMENITIES REFRESH THE SPIRIT.

DESIGN FIRM › Arias Associates
ART DIRECTORS › Mauricio Arias, Maral Sarkis
DESIGNERS › Mauricio Arias, Maral Sarkis
COPYWRITER › Dawn Mortensen
CLIENT › Hotel Casa Del Mar
TOOLS (SOFTWARE/PLATFORM) › QuarkXPress, Photoshop, Illustrator
PAPER STOCK › Mohawk superfine and McCoy silk
PRINTING PROCESS › Lithography, embossing and letterpress

DESIGN FIRM > Arias Associates
ART DIRECTORS > Mauricio Arias, Maral Sarkis, Steve Mortensen, Stephanie Yee
DESIGNERS > Mauricio Arias, Maral Sarkis, Steve Mortensen, Stephanie Yee
ILLUSTRATOR/PHOTOGRAPHER > Fred Licht
COPYWRITER > Words by Design
CLIENT > Crescent Heights
TOOLS (SOFTWARE/PLATFORM) > QuarkXPress, Photoshop, Illustrator
PAPER STOCK > Starwhite Vicksburg
PRINTING PROCESS > Lithography, letterpress

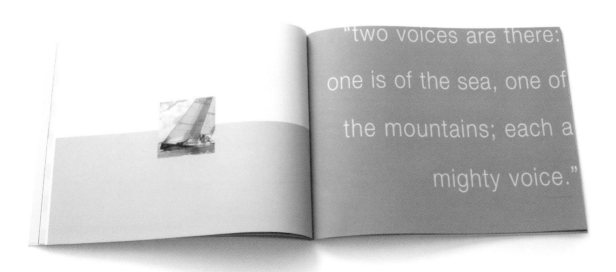

"two voices are there: one is of the sea, one of the mountains; each a mighty voice."

Anatomy of a *SmartSpiff*

When your Thoughtware calls for a *SmartSpiff* certificate, entry ticket or game piece, you can choose from many distinct constructions, shapes, sizes and materials. Design your *SmartSpiff* to adhere to your packaging with security features, or seal it in food barrier wrap for insertion with your product, or include a multi-fold brochure in your construction, or die cut a shape relating to your campaign's theme—virtually *anything* is possible.

The most cost-efficient construction is a two-ply, dry-seal rectangular format that peels apart and yields four copy panels. At right is an example shown at actual size.

10

DESIGN FIRM > Aspen Interactive
ART DIRECTOR > Ken Weightman
DESIGNER > Ken Weightman
CLIENT > Phoneworks
TOOLS (SOFTWARE/PLATFORM) > QuarkXPress, Adobe Photoshop, Macintosh
PAPER STOCK/PRINTING PROCESS > Four-color process and one match color

DESIGN FIRM › McMonigle & Associates
ART DIRECTOR › Jamie McConigle
DESIGNER › John Edwards
ILLUSTRATOR/PHOTOGRAPHER › Jamie McMonigle
COPYWRITER › Katrin Seher
CLIENT › Wescorp Investment Services
PAPER STOCK › Classic Crest

DESIGN FIRM › AXIS Communications
ART DIRECTOR › Craig Byers
DESIGNER › Craig Byers
ILLUSTRATOR/PHOTOGRAPHER › Thomas Arledge
CLIENT › Thomas Arledge
TOOLS (SOFTWARE/PLATFORM) › QuarkXPress, Macintosh
PAPER STOCK › Donside Gleneagle 100 lb. gloss, Proterra Kraft antique
PRINTING PROCESS › Four-color process

DESIGN FIRM › Sayles Graphic Design
ART DIRECTOR › John Sayles
DESIGNER › John Sayles
PHOTOGRAPHERS › David Crosby, Tony Smith
ILLUSTRATOR › John Sayles
COPYWRITER › Wendy Lyons
CLIENT › Greenville South Carolina Convention & Visitors Bureau
TOOLS (SOFTWARE/PLATFORM) › QuarkXPress, Macintosh
PRINTING PROCESS › Offset printed, includes tipped-on samples

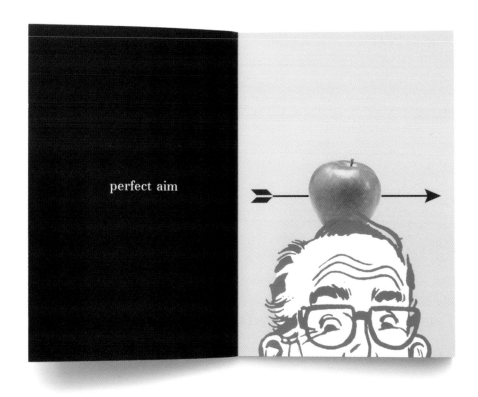

perfect aim

perfect fit

DESIGN FIRM › Sibley Peteet Design
ART DIRECTOR › Donna Aldridge
DESIGNER › Donna Aldridge
ILLUSTRATOR › Brandon Kirk
COPYWRITER › Don Sibley
CLIENT › Williamson Printing Company
TOOLS (SOFTWARE/PLATFORM) › QuarkXPress, Macintosh
PAPER STOCK › Strobe

WE'RE BECOMING MORE CUSTOMER FOCUSED UP AND DOWN THE LINE.
The big picture.
Creative thinking. Creative solutions.
Faster to market.
Of the 4,635 parts on this car, which is the most important?
Mine.

WE'RE NOT JUST DELIVERING GOODS, WE'RE DELIVERING SOLUTIONS.
Flexible shipping for inflexible schedules.
Innovative solutions for cool customers.
Linking the nation's largest retail chain.
IN MY BUSINESS TIME IS MONEY.
IF YOU'RE MAKING EXCUSES YOU'RE NOT MAKING MONEY

DESIGN FIRM › Witherspoon Advertising
ART DIRECTOR › Alan Comtois
DESIGNER › Alan Comtois
COPYWRITER › Carol Glover
CLIENT › Burlington Northern Railroad
TOOLS (SOFTWARE/PLATFORM) › QuarkXPress, Photoshop, Macintosh
PAPER STOCK › Signature

DESIGN FIRM › Peterson & Co.
ART DIRECTOR › Nhan T. Pham
DESIGNER › Nhan T. Pham
ILLUSTRATORS/PHOTOGRAPHERS › Various
COPYWRITER › In-house
CLIENT › Meeting Professionals International
TOOLS (SOFTWARE/PLATFORM) › Quark 4.0, Illustrator 8.0, Photoshop 5.0
PAPER STOCK › Tierra 110 lb. Starwhite velum cover plus mac flat form

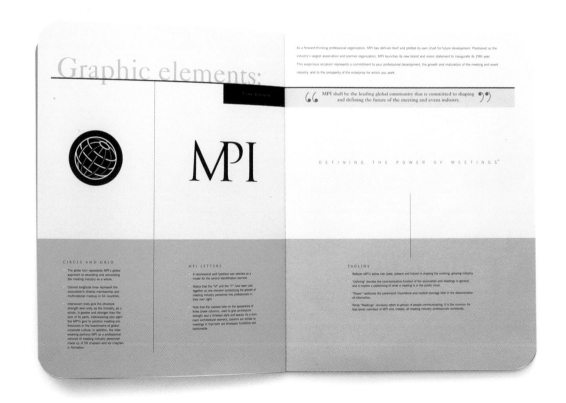

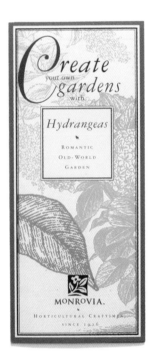

DESIGN FIRM › Erbe Design
ART DIRECTOR › Maureen Erbe
DESIGNER › Maureen Erbe
ILLUSTRATOR › Allison Starcher
COPYWRITER › Maureen Gilmer
CLIENT › Monrovia
TOOLS (SOFTWARE/PLATFORM) › QuarkXPress
PRINTING PROCESS › Lithography

Two Thousand Pounds

Two Thousand Pounds of Lead

Two Thousand Reasons to Keep on Trying

DESIGN FIRM > RBMM
ART DIRECTOR > Kenny Garrison
DESIGNER > Jim Jacobs
ILLUSTRATOR/PHOTOGRAPHER > Pete Lacker
COPYWRITER > Jim Jacobs
CLIENT > Williamson Printing Corp.
TOOLS (SOFTWARE/PLATFORM) > QuarkXPress, Photoshop

six compelling reasons to work with

sixredmarbles

| 1 | 2 | 3 | 4 | 5 | 6

DESIGN FIRM > Stoltze Design
ART DIRECTOR > Clifford Stoltze
DESIGNERS > Stacy Day, Brandon Blangger, Cynthia Patten
CLIENT > Six Red Marbles

DESIGN FIRM › Summa Comunicació
ART DIRECTORS › Wladimir Marnich, Griselda Marti
DESIGNERS › Wladimir Marnich, Griselda Marti
ILLUSTRATOR/PHOTOGRAPHER › Jose Luis Merino
COPYWRITER › Summa Comunicació - Espacio Pyme
CLIENT › Espacio Pyme
TOOLS (SOFTWARE/PLATFORM) › Freehand
PAPER STOCK › Uncoated stock
PRINTING PROCESS › Offset

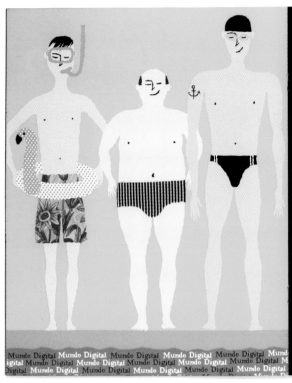

A quién nos dirigimos. www.espaciopyme.com se ha creado para satisfacer las necesidades de un mercado dinámico formado por numerosas pymes de multiples **sectores**. Nuestro proyecto se dirige a todas aquellas empresas con predisposición al cambio y con voluntad de apostar por las nuevas tecnologías e Internet como medio de futuro. Por ello, ofrecemos asesoramiento y soluciones a empresas con diferentes

niveles

de conocimiento y experiencia en la Red: tanto a empresas debutantes como a aquéllas que tienen un grado de familiarización medio con las nuevas tecnologías. A todas ellas, Espacio Pyme les ofrece su **ayuda** en este proceso de adaptación.

Qué es Espacio Pyme. Un espacio virtual donde las pequeñas y medianas empresas podrán aprovecharse de las ventajas que el **mundo digital** supone para su negocio y encontrar, en una única web, un acceso directo a una extensa oferta de **soluciones.** www.espaciopyme.com ha sido creado con un objetivo muy claro:

acercar

las nuevas tecnologías a las pymes y poner a su disposición información, servicios y herramientas que las ayuden a ser más competitivas. Confiar en Espacio Pyme significa obtener un conjunto de **ventajas** gracias a una amplia oferta de servicios de alta calidad y a bajo coste, ventajas que, hasta el día de hoy, estaban reservadas exclusivamente a las grandes empresas.

Nuevas Tecnologías

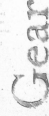

DESIGN FIRM › Hornall Anderson Design Works, Inc.
ART DIRECTOR › Jack Anderson
DESIGNERS › Jack Anderson, Belinda Bowling, Andrew Smith, Ed Lee
ILLUSTRATOR › Jack Unruh
COPYWRITERS › Various
CLIENT › Streamworks
TOOLS (SOFTWARE/PLATFORM) › QuarkXPress, Photoshop
PAPER STOCK › French Speckletone Kraft cover, natural text

DESIGN FIRM > Lee Reedy Creative
ART DIRECTOR > Lee Reedy
DESIGNER > Lee Reedy
ILLUSTRATOR/PHOTOGRAPHER > Stock
COPYWRITER > Suzy Patterson
CLIENT > Travel Connections
TOOLS (SOFTWARE/PLATFORM) > QuarkXPress
PAPER STOCK > Chipboard
PRINTING PROCESS > Two-color

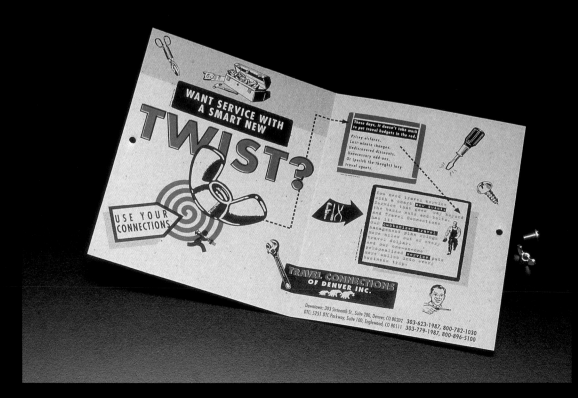

DESIGN FIRM › DBD International, Ltd
ART DIRECTOR › David Brier
DESIGNER › David Brier
ILLUSTRATOR › David Brier
PHOTOGRAPHER › Fredrik Broden
COPYWRITER › Steve Ferry
CLIENT › Rubin Baum
TOOLS (SOFTWARE/PLATFORM) › Macintosh, QuarkXPress, Illustrator
PAPER STOCK › Potlatch McCoy
PRINTING PROCESS › Four-color

these high-profile areas, our substantial background and sensitivity in dealing with the media on behalf of our clients help to minimize or avoid unwanted publicity.

Intellectual Property Litigation Substantially reinforced by the addition of the attorneys of the former Gold, Farrell & Marks, our firm's intellectual property lawyers bring unparalleled expertise to bear in handling the full range of litigation matters relating to trademarks, Internet domain names, copyrights, unfair competition, false advertising, rights of publicity and trade secrets.

Product Liability, Tort Defense and Professional Liability Litigation Insurance carriers and self-insureds retain RubinBaum to defend tort, product liability and professional liability actions, based on our considerable experience in general liability litigation. Our group has special expertise in litigation relating to asbestos injuries, premises liability, product liability and employers' liability (sexual harassment and discrimination). Our asbestos defense practice is one of the largest in the nation. RubinBaum has served as counsel in matters involving municipal employees (police, highway, fire, transportation), construction, directors and officers, errors and omissions, and professional liability (architects, engineers, accountants and lawyers). We have represented several prestigious New York law firms and a distinguished English firm of solicitors.

REAL ESTATE

Noted for our wide-ranging practice and ability to handle complex multi-disciplinary transactions, our real estate group represents clients in connection with acquisitions and sales of office properties, shopping centers, multifamily developments and commercial mortgage loan portfolios. We have extensive experience handling equity and debt financings, low-income housing and historic rehabilitation tax credit transactions, sale and leaseback transactions, site assemblages and ground and space lease transactions.

RubinBaum's clients include domestic and foreign property owners, developers, lending institutions, retail chains, private investors, cooperative apartment corporations and condominium associations. We also have an active practice in the representation of real estate opportunity funds, as well as foreign and domestic institutional and private owners and devel-

opers, including owners of trophy office properties in Manhattan and elsewhere. Our real estate group frequently joins with members of the corporate and tax departments to develop sophisticated multi-venture structures.

INTERNET LAW

Embracing new technologies is not new for RubinBaum. Our experience in media related matters in particular goes back to 1961. Paralleling the exponential growth in the media and telecommunications industries, RubinBaum's exceptional background uniquely positions the firm to service companies involved in e-commerce, web publishing and technology development in all life-cycle phases. We advise Internet start-up businesses, including assisting the founders with venture capital sources, preparing private placement memoranda, analyzing competing offers and preparing stock purchase agreements.

After the completion of the organization and financing of start-ups, the focus of our representation shifts to guidance relating to operational and employment issues. Our firm provides advice regarding agreements for web site development, use of content providers, web site hosting services, and formation of affiliate relationships between site owners and advertising representatives.

Our attorneys offer considerable expertise in technology licensing agreements, licensing of patents, copyrights, and trademarks, antitrust counseling, and litigation applicable to the Internet.

INTELLECTUAL PROPERTY

In addition to intellectual property litigation expertise, our firm has substantial experience in counseling clients in the clearance, acquisition, disposition, registration, maintenance, protection and licensing of trademarks, Internet domain names, copyrights, advertising claims, rights of publicity and trade secrets. Our practice includes representation of clients in the fields of book packaging and publishing, computer software development, cosmetics, clothing, chemicals, e-commerce, telemarketing, jewelry, ware making, art, television, cable, film, music, publishing and recording. RubinBaum's lawyers also advise clients in patent licensing, franchising and related areas.

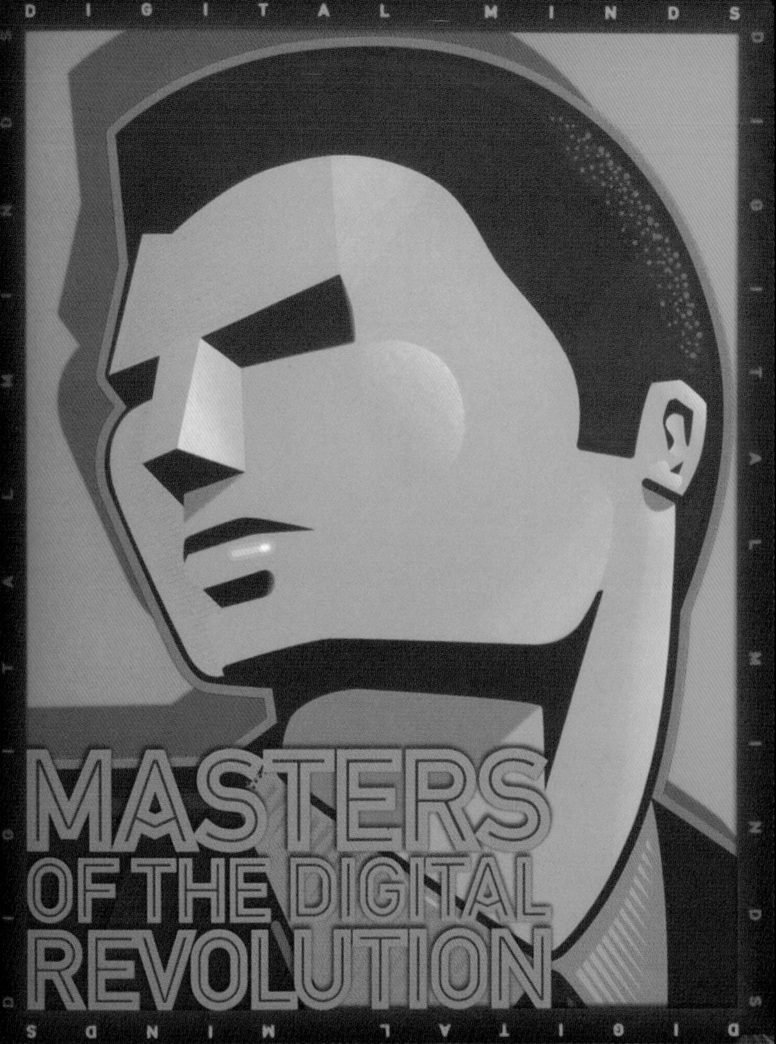
DIGITAL MINDS
MASTERS
OF THE DIGITAL
REVOLUTION

THE NEW STANDARD It's not about which platform or manufacturer. It's about you, greater control, and limitless compatibility, across the hall — or across the globe. You're entering the first DIGITAL platform-compatible world of technology. Be wary of "computer resellers" who try to pitch other alternatives. As a pro-active technology supplier, Digital Minds is now offering the future and the way work will be done, rather than merely providing tomorrow's soon-to-be-extinct rave. Imagine: conflict-free workflow... platform to platform. It's almost as unbelievable as world peace. MINDS

DESIGN FIRM > DBD International, Ltd.
ART DIRECTOR > David Brier
DESIGNER > David Brier
ILLUSTRATOR > David Brier
PHOTOGRAPHER > Jake Armour
COPYWRITER > David Brier
CLIENT > Digital Minds
TOOLS (SOFTWARE/PLATFORM) > Macintosh, QuarkXPress, Illustrator
PRINTING PROCESS > Color process, vintage gloss and delustered polymer laminate

opportuni-
ties in
life
are very
rare, and I
thank you

NONPROFIT, EDUCATIONAL, INSTITUTIONAL + HEALTHCARE **BROCHURES**

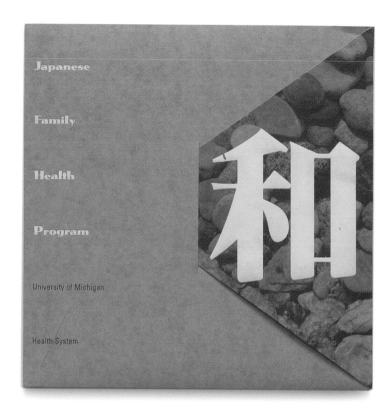

DESIGN FIRM › Wagner Design
ART DIRECTORS › Laura Herold, Kazuko Sacks
DESIGNER › Jill Wagner
COPYWRITER › Toni Voss
CLIENT › University of Michigan, Department of Family Medicine,
Japanese Family Health Program
TOOLS (SOFTWARE/PLATFORM) › QuarkXPress, Photoshop
PAPER STOCK › Folder: Neenah Environment Sedona red, 80 lb. cover;
Insert: Warren Lustre dull cream, 80 lb. cover
PRINTING PROCESS › Inserts: four-color; folder: one spot color plus foil stamp

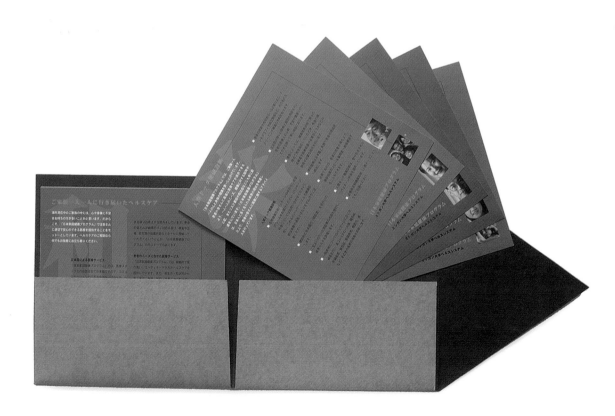

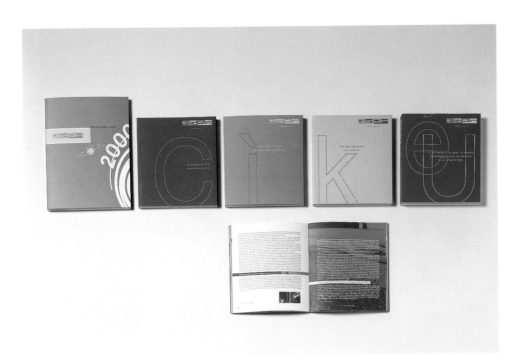

DESIGN FIRM > Didier Saco Design
ART DIRECTOR > Didier Saco
DESIGNER > Laurent Dumte
ILLUSTRATOR/PHOTOGRAPHER > Cendrine ronsard
CLIENT > Festival D'Art Lyrique Aiten Provence
PAPER STOCK > Verge 110 grammes

DESIGN FIRM > Giovanni Design Associates
ART DIRECTORS > John Frontino, Edward Maichin
DESIGNERS > John Frontino, Edward Maichin
ILLUSTRATOR/PHOTOGRAPHER > Stock
COPYWRITER > Advertising Council
CLIENT > Advertising Council
TOOLS (SOFTWARE/PLATFORM) > QuarkXPress, Photoshop

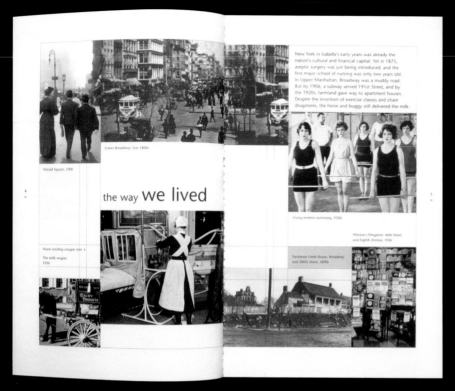

New York in Isabella's early years was already the nation's cultural and financial capital. Yet in 1875, aseptic surgery was just being introduced, and the first major school of nursing was only two years old. In Upper Manhattan, Broadway was a muddy road. But by 1906, a subway served 191st Street, and by the 1920s, farmland gave way to apartment houses. Despite the invention of exercise classes and chain drugstores, the horse and buggy still delivered the milk.

Lower Broadway, late 1800s

Herald Square, 1906

the way we lived

Young women exercising, 1920s

Nurse tending oxygen tent ›

The milk wagon, 1936

Whelan's Drugstore, 44th Street and Eighth Avenue, 1936

Dyckman Farm House, Broadway and 204th Street, 1890s

DESIGN FIRM › O & J Design Inc.
ART DIRECTORS › Barbara Olejniczak, Lia Camera Mariscal
DESIGNERS › Barbara Olejniczak, Lia Camera Mariscal
ILLUSTRATOR/PHOTOGRAPHER › David Radler
COPYWRITERS › Kalen Blinn, Mimi Koren
CLIENT › Isabella Geriatric Center
TOOLS (SOFTWARE/PLATFORM) › QuarkXpress
PAPER STOCK/PRINTING PROCESS › Cover: three-color; interior: two-color

DESIGN FIRM › Zappata Diseñadores S.C.
ART DIRECTOR › Ibo Angulo
DESIGNER › Ibo Angulo
CLIENT › Nuevo Mundo University
TOOLS (SOFTWARE/PLATFORM) › Photoshop, Freehand, Macintosh
PRINTING PROCESS › Offset, couche

DESIGN FIRM > Oh Boy, A Design Company

ART DIRECTOR > David Salanitro

DESIGNER > Ryan Mahar

PHOTOGRAPHER > Scott Goldsmith

COPYWRITERS > Susan Wilkinson, Dana Cooper-The Doctors' Company

CLIENT > The Doctors' Company

PAPER STOCK > Superfine, ultra white smooth

DESIGN FIRM > Shamlian Advertising
ART DIRECTOR > Brian DiRienzi
DESIGNER > Brian DiRienzi
CLIENT > ESF Summer Camps
TOOLS (SOFTWARE/PLATFORM) > Photoshop, Macintosh
PAPER STOCK/PRINTING PROCESS > 4/4

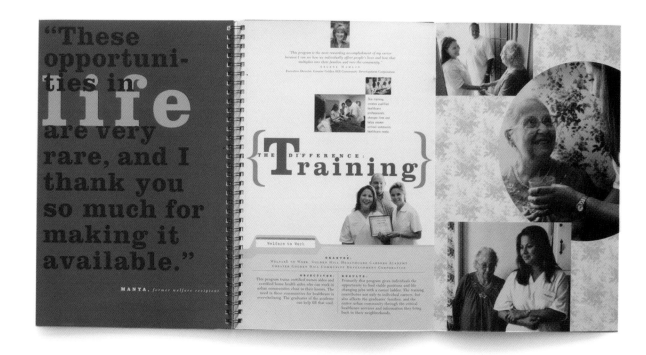

DESIGN FIRM > Gee + Chung Design
ART DIRECTOR > Earl Gee
DESIGNERS > Earl Gee, Fani Chung
PHOTOGRAPHER > Steve Jost
COPYWRITERS > Stephanie Lasenza, Gary Hawk
CLIENT > Alliance Healthcare Foundation
TOOLS (SOFTWARE/PLATFORM) > QuarkXPress, Adobe Illustrator, Photoshop
PAPER STOCK > Potlatch Karma natural 100 lb. text, French Paper Co., Speckletone Madero beach white 70 lb. text
PRINTING PROCESS > Offset lithography, blind embossing

DESIGN FIRM > Parsons Promotion Design
ART DIRECTORS > Evelyn Kim, Meg Callery
DESIGNERS > Evelyn Kim, Meg Callery
ILLUSTRATOR/PHOTOGRAPHER > Marty Heitner
COPYWRITERS > Carole Schaffer, Hilary Howard
CLIENT > Parsons Undergraduate Catalog
TOOLS (SOFTWARE/PLATFORM) > QuarkXPress, Photoshop, Illustrator

DESIGN FIRM › The Art Institute of Seattle
ART DIRECTOR › Scott Engelhardt
DESIGNER › Scott Engelhardt
PHOTOGRAPHER › Zee Wendell
COPYWRITER › Susan Goschie
CLIENT › The Art Institute of Seattle
TOOLS (SOFTWARE/PLATFORM) › Macintosh, QuarkXPress
PAPER STOCK › Cougar opaque
PRINTING PROCESS › Sheet fed

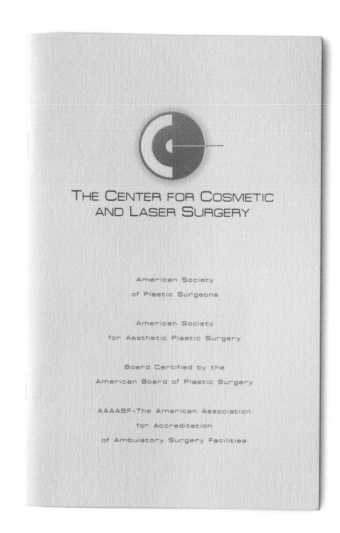

DESIGN FIRM › Griffin Design
ART DIRECTOR › Tracy Griffin Sleeter
DESIGNER › Tracy Griffin Sleeter
ILLUSTRATOR › Rick Kessinger
PHOTOGRAPHER › Stock photography
COPYWRITER › Cindy Lorimor
CLIENT › Center for Cosmetic & Laser Surgery
TOOLS (SOFTWARE/PLATFORM) › Macintosh
PRINTING PROCESS › Offset with aqueous coating, embossed foil stamp, Bloomington Offset Process, Inc.

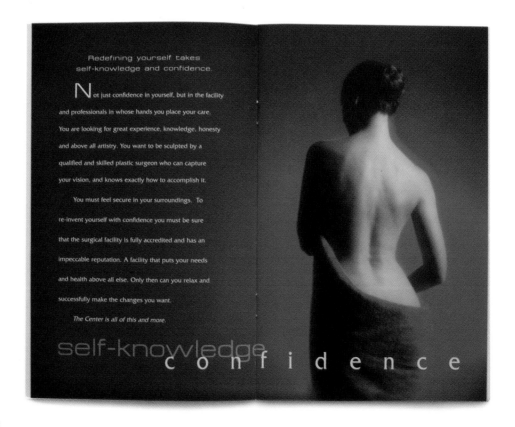

www.thap.net

path!

DESIGN FIRM › Oh Boy, A Design Company
ART DIRECTOR › David Salanitro
DESIGNER › Alice Chang
PHOTOGRAPHER › Tony Stone Images
COPYWRITER › Son Rant
CLIENT › Thap!
PAPER STOCK › Caress eggshell 80 lb.
PRINTING PROCESS › Offset, sheet fed

!augh

Laugh and the whole world laughs with you. Laughing relaxes muscles, increases heart rate, improves the oxygenation of blood and releases positive mood-enhancing endorphins which all lead to longer, healthier and happier lives.

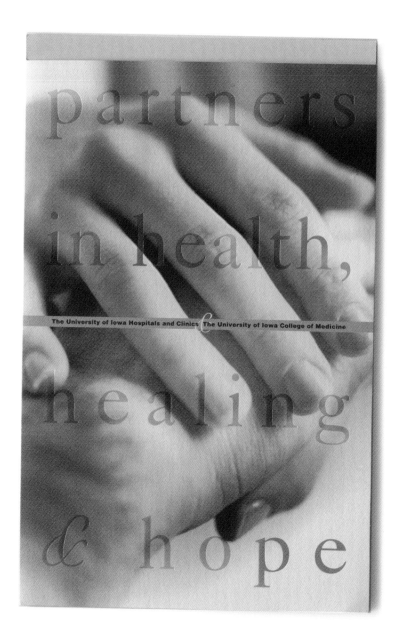

DESIGN FIRM > University of Iowa Foundation
ART DIRECTOR > Theresa Black
DESIGNER > Theresa Black
ILLUSTRATORS/PHOTOGRAPHERS > Jon Van Allen, Diane Hill, Reggie Morrow
COPYWRITER > Claudia Reinhardt
CLIENT > VI Foundation
TOOLS (SOFTWARE/PLATFORM) > Pagemaker, Photoshop, Macintosh
PAPER STOCK > Gilbert Voice
PRINTING PROCESS > Three PMS colors

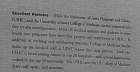

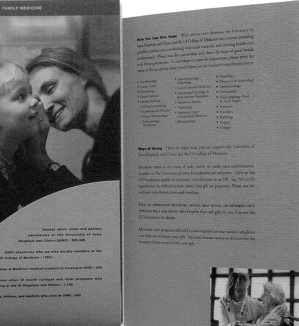

FAMILY MEDICINE

Excellent Partners While the University of Iowa Hospitals and Clinics (UIHC) and the University of Iowa College of Medicine operate independently, they are also interdependent. Most UI medical students and students in other health care programs have their first patient care experiences at UIHC. In addition to teaching and conducting research, College of Medicine faculty make up the medical staff at UIHC where they treat patients. Each year UIHC is listed among America's top 20 hospitals—with several departments ranked in the top 20 nationally. The UIHC and the UI College of Medicine share staff, space, and missions.

Contributions from individuals and organizations are vital to the continuing excellence of these institutions.

What is a teaching hospital, and why is it different? Teaching hospitals are at the heart of modern academic medicine and the main source of new medical treatments and techniques. Physicians and other health care professionals in community hospitals, clinics, and health care agencies look to the UI Hospitals and Clinics for specialized services.

UIHC serves as a training site for medical students and residents as well as dentists, nurses, medical technologists, pharmacists, physical therapists, and physician assistants. These highly motivated individuals in training enhance patient care and give patients special attention.

The missions of teaching hospitals like UIHC are patient care, research, and education, so they must maintain more staff and high-tech equipment than other hospitals. This puts them at a competitive disadvantage in the changing marketplace. To continue as leaders in modern health care, UIHC and other teaching hospitals must look to private contributions.

continuing excellence

Annual clinic visits and patient admissions at the University of Iowa Hospitals and Clinics (UIHC) : 500,000

UIHC physicians who are also faculty members at the UI College of Medicine : 100%

UI College of Medicine medical students in training at UIHC : 540

Students from other UI health colleges and other programs who receive training at the UI Hospitals and Clinics : 1,100

Medical residents, fellows, and dentists who train at UIHC : 645

How You Can Give Hope With private contributions, the University of Iowa Hospitals and Clinics and the UI College of Medicine can continue providing excellent patient care, conducting important research, and training health care professionals. Please join this partnership and share the hope of good health with future generations. To contribute to a specific department, please print the name of the area (from those listed below) on the enclosed contribution form:

- Anesthesiology
- Cancer Center
- Dermatology
- Family Medicine
- Internal Medicine
  - Allergy-Immunology
  - Cardiovascular Diseases
  - Clinical Pharmacology
  - Endocrinology-Metabolism
- Gastroenterology-Hepatology
- General Internal Medicine
- Hematology/Oncology & Bone Marrow Transplant
- Infectious Diseases
- Nephrology
- Pulmonary Care-Occupational Medicine
- Rheumatology
- Neurology
- Obstetrics & Gynecology
- Ophthalmology
- Orthopaedics
- Otolaryngology-Head & Neck Surgery
- Pediatrics
- Psychiatry
- Radiology
- Surgery
- Urology

Ways of Giving There are many ways you can support the University of Iowa Hospitals and Clinics and the UI College of Medicine.

OUTRIGHT GIFTS in the form of cash, check, or credit card authorization, (payable to The University of Iowa Foundation) are welcome. Gifts to the UI Foundation qualify as charitable contributions to an IRC Sec. 501(c)(3) organization for federal income, estate, and gift tax purposes. Please use the enclosed contribution form and envelope.

GIFTS OF APPRECIATED SECURITIES, STOCKS, REAL ESTATE, OR DEFERRED GIFTS THROUGH WILLS AND TRUSTS offer benefits that cash gifts do not. Contact the UI Foundation for details.

MATCHING GIFT programs offered by your employer or your spouse's employer may help you multiply your gift. See your human resources director for the necessary forms to send with your gift.

---

partners in health, healing & hope

share
learn
explore
care
hope
understand
believe

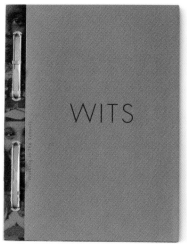

DESIGN FIRM > SamataMason
ART DIRECTOR > Greg Samata
DESIGNER > Kevin Kureger
PHOTOGRAPHERS > Sandro, Martha Brock
CLIENT > WITS (Working in the Schools)
TOOLS (SOFTWARE/PLATFORM) > QuarkXPress, Macintosh
PAPER STOCK > French Speckletone Chipboard,
Appleton Utopia two matt and Springhill Incentive
PRINTING PROCESS > Offset printing, sheet fed

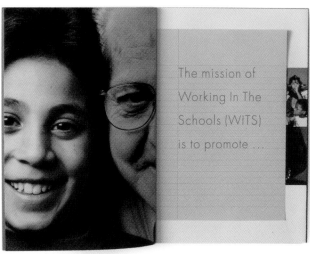

The mission of
Working In The
Schools (WITS)
is to promote . . . .

Being adopted

is like being a puzzle with

a missing piece.

DESIGN FIRM > AXIS Communications
ART DIRECTOR > Craig Byers
DESIGNER > Tamara Dowd
ILLUSTRATOR > Becky Heavner
PHOTOGRAPHER > Robert Burke
COPYWRITER > Kathy Mitchell, Tamara Dowd
CLIENT > The Center for Adoption Support and Education
TOOLS (SOFTWARE/PLATFORM) > QuarkXPress, Macintosh
PRINTING PROCESS > 4-color

american academy of microbiology

The American Academy of Microbiology is the honorific leadership group within the American Society for Microbiology (ASM), the world's oldest and largest life science organization. The mission of the American Academy of Microbiology is to recognize scientists for outstanding contributions to microbiology and provide microbiological expertise in the service of science and the public.

The Academy serves as a resource to governmental agencies, industry, ASM, and the larger scientific and lay communities by convening colloquia to address critical issues in microbiology. The Academy brings together a group of scientific experts for several days of structured, directed deliberations, resulting in an analytical, practical, objective report that is widely disseminated.

The Academy, through its sponsorship of the American College of Microbiology, certifies outstanding microbiologists in clinical and industrial specialties and accredits postdoctoral training programs in clinical and public health microbiology and immunology. The Academy also manages a stellar awards program, recognizing achievement and potential in all areas of microbiology.

DESIGN FIRM > Pensaré Design Group, Ltd.
ART DIRECTOR > Mary Ellen Vehlow
DESIGNER > Kundia D. Wood
ILLUSTRATOR/PHOTOGRAPHER > Photodisc Stock Photography
COPYWRITERS > Carol Colgan, American Academy of Microbiology
CLIENT > American Academy of Microbiology
TOOLS (SOFTWARE/PLATFORM) > Photoshop, QuarkXPress, Macintosh
PAPER STOCK/PRINTING PROCESS > Neenah U.V. ultra, Neenah Classic Crest

Utbildningens mål

Vem vänder sig linjen till

Linjens struktur och innehåll

Ytterligare information

Kursmoment

Ingenjörsvetenskap

Rymdteknik

20 POÄNG – HALVFART

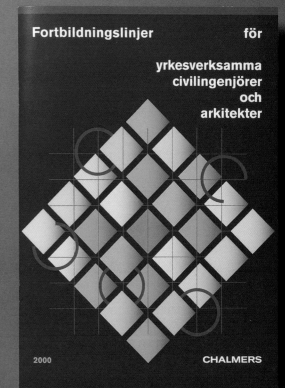

Fortbildningslinjer för

yrkesverksamma
civilingenjörer
och
arkitekter

2000

CHALMERS

DESIGN FIRM > Göthberg + Co. Design
ART DIRECTOR > Bengt Göthberg
DESIGNER > Bengt Göthberg
ILLUSTRATOR > Bengt Göthberg
PHOTOGRAPHER > Jens Karlsson
CLIENT > Chalmers Tekniskr Hogsköla
PAPER STOCK > Woodfree uncoated

DESIGN FIRM > Erbe Design
ART DIRECTOR > Maureen Erbe
DESIGNER > Maureen Erbe
ILLUSTRATOR/PHOTOGRAPHER > Scott Streble
COPYWRITER > Victoria Thurlough
CLIENT > Huntington Hospital
TOOLS (SOFTWARE/PLATFORM) > QuarkXPress
PRINTING PROCESS > Lithography

DESIGN FIRM > Gardner Design
ART DIRECTOR > Brian Miller
DESIGNER > Travis Brown
CLIENT > Kansas Joint Replacement Institute
TOOLS (SOFTWARE/PLATFORM) > Freehand, Photoshop
PRINTING PROCESS > Four-color

DESIGN FIRM > Danette Angerer
ART DIRECTOR > Danette Angerer
DESIGNER > Danette Angerer
ILLUSTRATORS/PHOTOGRAPHERS > Mike Schlotterback, Mark Trade, Rod Bradley, Michael Ask, Jeff Schmatt
COPYWRITER > Elinor Day
CLIENT > Brucemore
TOOLS (SOFTWARE/PLATFORM) > Pagemaker, Macintosh
PAPER STOCK > Dust cover: Environment Desert Storm. Cover: Environment Sedona Red.
Flysheet: U.V./Ultra II sepia interior. Interior stock: Sterling satin.
PRINTING PROCESS > Four-color process, PMS 876 metallic and spot dull varnish
PRINTER > Garner Printing, Des Moines, IA

Different Drugs
ALCOHOL

Other names:

Ale, beer, booze, drink, plonk, sherbet, spirits, wine.

Under the influence...

Off your head/face, pissed, sozzled, drunk, stoned, tiddly, tipsy.

Background information:

Alcoholic drinks are produced by the process of fermenting fruit, grain or vegetables to produce an intoxicating drink which may vary in alcohol content. Distillation of the fermented product produces spirits with a higher concentration of alcohol.

How it is taken:

Alcohol is usually swallowed as a drink.

Effects and risks:

Alcohol is a depressant drug which slows down the Central Nervous System.
Small amounts: remove inhibitions, relaxes.
Large amounts: loss of co-ordination, slurred speech, double vision, nausea and/or vomiting,
Very large amounts: unconsciousness, possible heart attack, coma or death.

Alcohol is rapidly absorbed into the blood stream. The first effects are almost immediate and vary greatly depending on how much is taken, how quickly it is drunk, body weight, age and sex, *(alcohol affects women more than it affects men)*, and whether other drugs have been taken or food eaten.

A tolerance to alcohol and possibly dependence may develop with sustained use. Sudden withdrawal from severe alcohol dependence can be life threatening. Physical effects of prolonged heavy use include an increased risk of liver cirrhosis, stomach ulcers, cancers of the mouth, stomach and throat, heart disease, pancreatitis, brain damage and destruction of nerve cells.

Excessive regular drinking commonly aggravates family, personal and financial problems. *(see **Drug Problems** for more detailed information).*

Legal status:

Alcohol may only be sold under licence to a person over the age of 18 but may be drunk by anyone (see **Drugs and the Law** for more detailed information).

Did you know?

Regular consumption in excess of the daily benchmarks of 3-4 units a day for men and 2-3 units a day for women may cause significant health risks.

---
1 UNIT IS EQUAL TO

| Half a pint of ordinary beer, lager or cider | Quarter of a pint of strong beer, lager or cider | One small glass of wine, sherry or port | One 25ml measure of spirit or liqueur |

a parent's guide to drugs

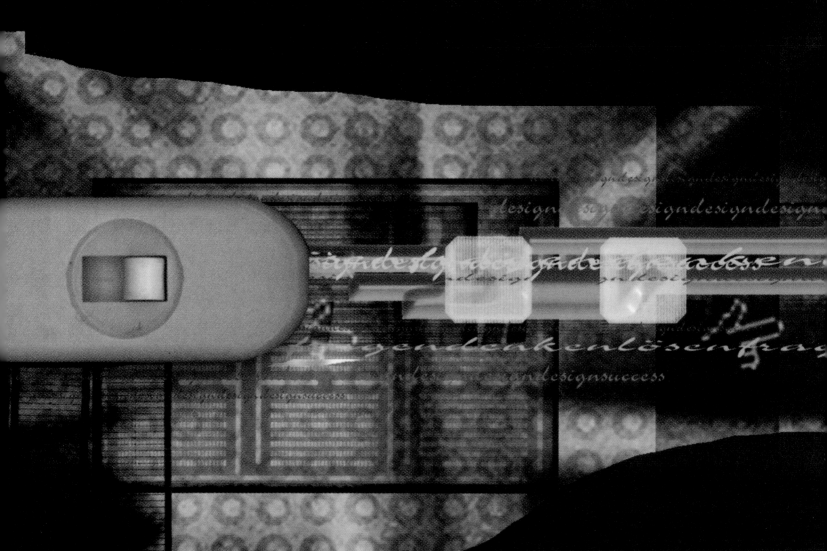

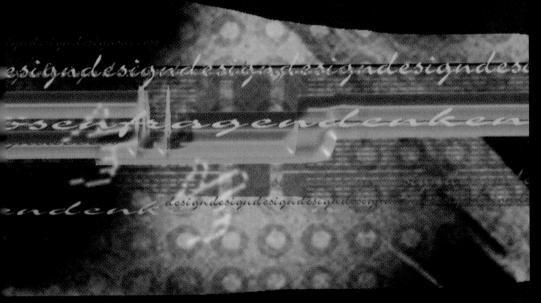

SELF-PROMOTIONAL BROCHURES

DESIGN FIRM › Emery Vincent Design
ART DIRECTOR › Garry Emery
DESIGNER › Emery Vincent Design
CLIENT › Emery Vincent Design
TOOLS (SOFTWARE/PLATFORM) › QuarkXPress, Illustrator, Photoshop

I have never seen the practice as part of the mainstream, nor as part of the avant garde, but as occupying some sort of curious middle ground, with a keen interest in new media and the digital future. There is no special focus on two-, three- or four-dimensional design, simply a general interest in each. Similarly there is equal commitment to large, small and middle-sized projects, as well as an interest in both the cultural and the commercial – although to every commercial project we endeavour to bring a cultural dimension. Our practice happily occupies its own territory.

04
The work

My background is that of a traditional typographer, influenced by modernism and calligraphy (in particular the calligraphy of Edward Johnson)

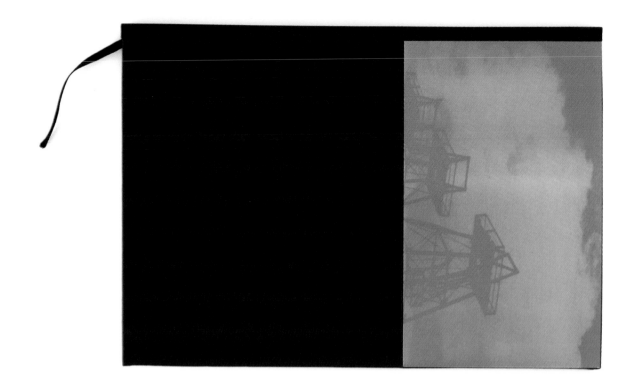

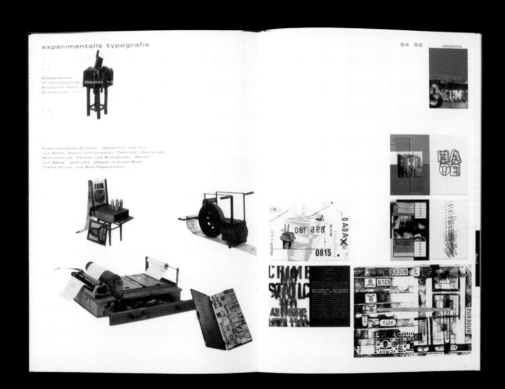

DESIGN FIRM > Magma
ART DIRECTORS > Lars Harmsen, Axel Brinkman, Uli Weiss
DESIGNERS > Lars Harmsen, Axel Brinkman, Uli Weiss
CLIENT > Magma

DESIGN FIRM › Graif Design
ART DIRECTOR › Matt Graif
DESIGNER › Matt Graif
CLIENT › Seven Course Design
TOOLS (SOFTWARE/PLATFORM) › Illustrator 9.0
PAPER STOCK › Neenah Paper Co.
PRINTING PROCESS › Offset printing

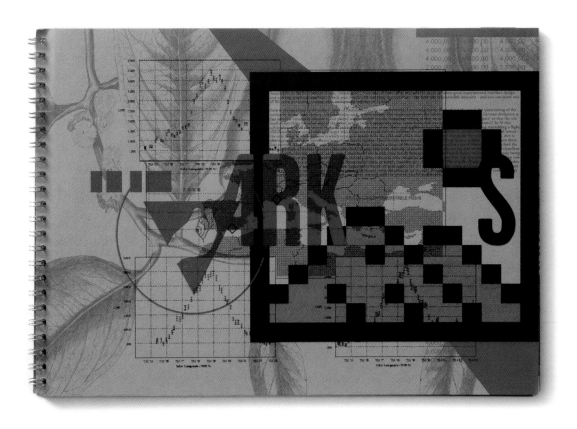

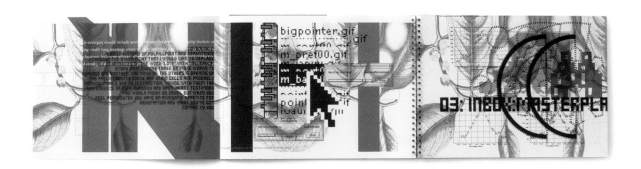

DESIGN FIRM > Fork Unstable Media GMBH

ART DIRECTOR > David Linderman

DESIGNER > David Linderman

COPYWRITER > David Linderman

CLIENT > Fork Unstable Media

TOOLS (SOFTWARE/PLATFORM) > Freehand 8.0, Photoshop 5.5, Capture v 4.0, Macintosh platform

PAPER STOCK > Gmund "Havanna," Munken "Munken Pur"

PRINTING PROCESS > Three-color, U.V. glaze

DESIGN FIRM > Pepe Gimeno - Proyecto Gráfico
ART DIRECTOR > Pepe Gimeno
DESIGNERS > Suso Pérez, José P. Gill
CLIENT > Pepe Gimeno - Proyecto Gráfico
TOOLS (SOFTWARE/PLATFORM) > Freehand 8.0, Photo
PRINTING PROCESS > Offset

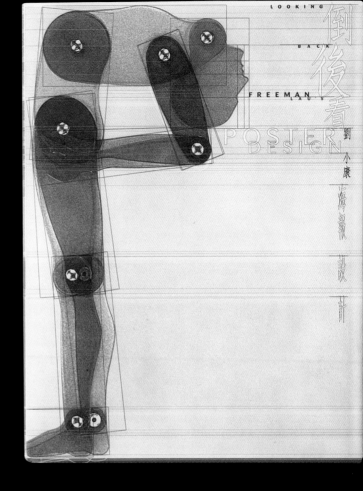

倒後看 劉小康海報設計

DESIGN FIRM › Kan & Lau Design Consultants
ART DIRECTOR › Freeman Lau Siu Hong
DESIGNER › Freeman Lau Siu Hong
CLIENT › Kan & Lau Design Consultants
TOOLS (SOFTWARE/PLATFORM) › Freehand 8.0, Photoshop 5.0
PAPER STOCK › 157 Gulliver

The 10th Hong Kong Print
Awards Invitational Poster
Exhibition

Computers and photocopiers
have experimentation of ideas
so much easier these days.
These designs on a simple idea
were tested this time: printing
technology spreads different
cultures, allowing different races
to understand each other and
come together. But this time I
gave up my favourite design cup
and opted for a more widely
accepted layout as the final
design shot. The remaining one
bottom, which seems to resemble
the style of another designer, plus
the fact that its layout was too
plain, was simply not considered.

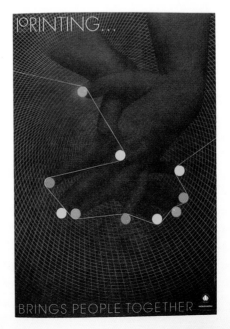

第十屆香港印製大獎
海報設計邀請展

DESIGN FIRM > Libby Perszyk Kathman
ART DIRECTOR > Matt Baughan
DESIGNER > Matt Baughan
ILLUSTRATORS/PHOTOGRAPHERS > Brad Holland, Jeff Kauck, Dane Heithaus, Greg Kuchik
COPYWRITER > John Recker
CLIENT > Libby Perszyk Kathman
TOOLS (SOFTWARE/PLATFORM) > Illustrator, Photoshop, Macintosh
PAPER STOCK > 100 lb. centura gloss cover and text
PRINTING PROCESS > Offset

DESIGN FIRM › IE Design

ART DIRECTOR › Marcie Carson

DESIGNER › Marcie Carson

ILLUSTRATOR/PHOTOGRAPHER › Kevin Merrill

COPYWRITER › Marcie Carson

CLIENT › IE Design

TOOLS (SOFTWARE/PLATFORM) › Macintosh, Illustrator, Photoshop, QuarkXPress

PAPER STOCK › Gilbert esse, Gilelcar Oxford

PRINTING PROCESS › Four-color

DESIGN FIRM › ARTiculation Group/Wilco Design
ART DIRECTORS › Joseph Chan, Wilson Lam
DESIGNERS › Joseph Chan, Wilson Lam, Helena Ng, Karin Fukuzawa
PHOTOGRAPHERS › Joseph Chan, Steven Chan, see spot run and various stock
COPYWRITERS › David Savoie, Pramila David
CLIENT › ARTiculation Group
TOOLS (SOFTWARE/PLATFORM) › Photoshop
PAPER STOCK › Strathmore

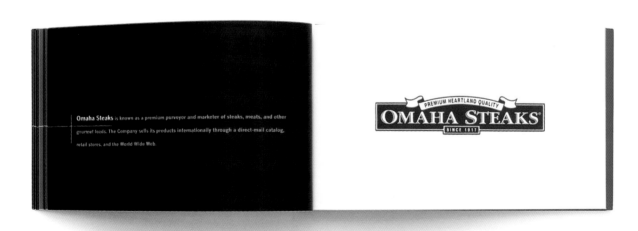

DESIGN FIRM > Fitch
ART DIRECTOR > Mark Uskavich
DESIGNER > Mark Uskavich
ILLUSTRATOR/PHOTOGRAPHER > Mark Uskavich
CLIENT > Fitch
PRINTING PROCESS > Baesman Printing

foco

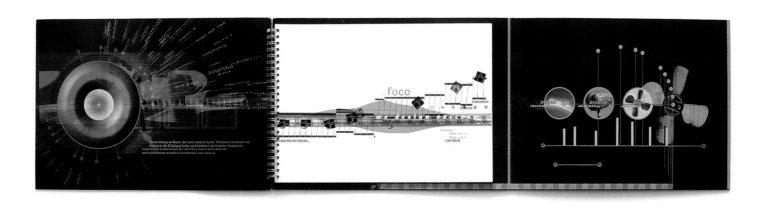

DESIGN FIRM **>** Foco Media gmbh & cte
ART DIRECTOR **>** Steffen Janus
DESIGNER **>** Steffen Janus
CLIENT **>** Foco Media gmbh & cte

DESIGN FIRM > Oh Boy, A Design Company
ART DIRECTOR > David Salanitro
DESIGNERS > Hunter Wimmer, Ted Bluey
PHOTOGRAPHER > Hunter Wimmer
COPYWRITERS > David Salanitro, Hunter Wimmer
CLIENT > Oh Boy, A Design Company
PAPER STOCK > Mohawk 65 lb. superfine, ultrawhite
PRINTING PROCESS > Offset, sheet fed

DESIGN FIRM > Witherspoon Advertising
ART DIRECTOR > Rishi Seth
DESIGNER > Rishi Seth
COPYWRITER > Rishi Seth
CLIENT > Witherspoon Advertising
TOOLS (SOFTWARE/PLATFORM) > QuarkXPress, Illustrator, Macintosh
PAPER STOCK > Starwhite Vicksburg
PRINTING PROCESS > Offset

Iomega: Zip, Clik!, and Jaz drives
Repositioning to create the future

As computer users become more sophisticated, they become more demanding – wanting affordable data storage systems with capacity to capture, share, organize, and protect all their business and personal 'stuff'.

The Iomega Corporation, an established leader in manufacturing removable data storage products, sought to move beyond their traditional business-to-business and professional market sectors. They briefed Fitch to reposition their brand and change the way consumers and the marketplace think about data storage products.

Research with both techno savvy and casual users showed that while portable data storage was something consumers needed and wanted, they felt alienated by marketing aimed at computer experts. The new brand positioning, packaging, and communications used straightforward language rather than technical jargon, and product names were kept short, fun, and memorable. Even the Iomega identity was given a lower case 'i' to make it friendlier.

Our research also uncovered several product voids in the market which led to the development of the original 100MB Zip drive. Subsequent product additions have included the Jaz, Ditto, Clik! and Zip 250 drives.

These products have enabled Iomega to deliver technology that not only addresses real user needs, but has also given our client ownership of an entirely new category of the computer peripherals market. In March 1999 Iomega announced that it had shipped 25 million Zip drives and 150 million disks to date, and the company currently commands 87% of the removable data storage market. Zip has become a generic household name – the Hoover of data storage.

25 Million Zip drives shipped to date

iomega zip 250
25 million
1

Consumers want useful, usable and desirable products – served by technology rather than driven by it

User Research
Consumer Research
Brand Strategy
Product Design
Engineering
Packaging
Graphic Design
Information Architecture
Information Design
User Interface Design
Naming
Video Graphics
Exhibition Design
Interactive Design
Programming

The Zip 250 offers two-and-a-half times the storage capacity of the original Zip drive.

Iomega packaging communicates product features and capabilities in easy-to-understand, non technical language.

The Iomega Clik! enables simple, fast transfer of digital image files.

DESIGN FIRM > Fitch
ART DIRECTOR > Carol Dean
DESIGNER > Nick Richards
COPYWRITER > Jennifer Wood
CLIENT > Fitch

Microsoft: Hermes Internet Telephone
The future of communication

The Market
- Research has shown that a product, and the experience of using a product, are inseparable. Most existing technology offers too many features, while consumers are actually looking for products that do fewer things better.
- Microsoft has made a commitment to offer internet technology products that not only integrate software innovations, but in their physical state, fulfil consumers' evolving needs.

The Challenge
- Develop concepts for internet appliances to combine different information, media and communication functions – including voicemail, caller ID, e-mail, telephone and Web access – in a single object.
- Develop a series of completely new touch screen user interfaces (UIs) to serve a range of business, family and personal uses.

The Work
- Taking into account both the user experience and the industrial design of the product, a user interface (UI) was developed that is intuitive and easy to navigate, while offering a comprehensive range of functions.
- Identification of three main user scenarios: kitchen (home), business and family room, plus design of UIs and product formats that answered the needs of each setting.

The Result
- The concepts developed were used to present a range of possible applications for Microsoft's software to internal management, and potential manufacturing partners.
- The components of the UI designs will be used as a base for Microsoft's future product development.

> ⚠ NASA spent $200 million on computers to put a man on the moon. Today the same technology costs $900.

The Hermes Internet Appliance screen – desktop configuration

Several conceptual hardware platforms were developed to suggest the unlimited range of usage applications

User interface for the Hermes phone application

In a world of technology overload, consumers are looking for products that do fewer things better

User Research
Consumer Research
Product Design
User Interface Design

DESIGN FIRM > Fitch
ART DIRECTOR > Vassoula Vasiliou
DESIGNER > Kian Kuan
CLIENT > Fitch

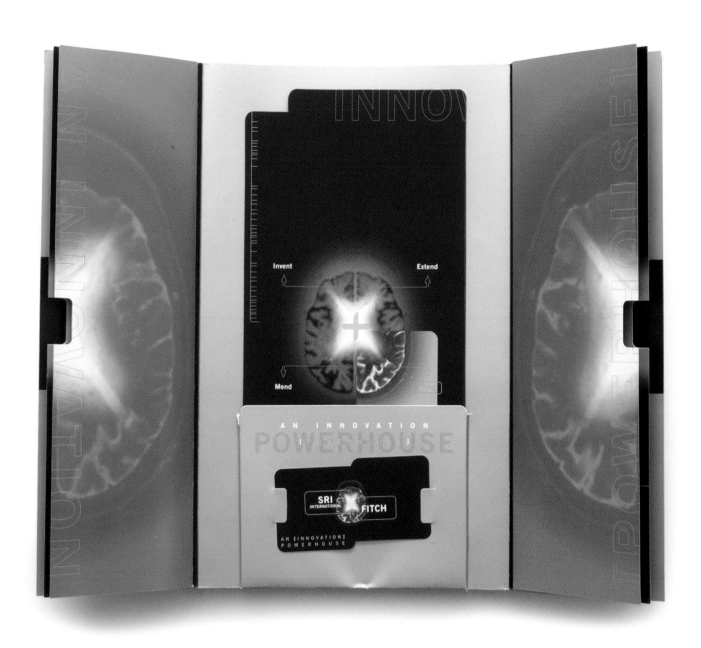

DESIGN FIRM > Louey/Rubino Design Group Inc.
ART DIRECTOR > Robert Louey
DESIGNERS > Robert Louey, Alex Chao, Anja Mueller
ILLUSTRATORS/PHOTOGRAPHERS > Eric Tucker, Jamey Stillings, Everard Williams Jr., Lise Metzger, Neal Brown, Ann Elliot Cutting, Hugh Kretschmer
COPYWRITER > Elisabeth Charney
CLIENT > Louey/Rubino Design Group
TOOLS (SOFTWARE/PLATFORM) > QuarkXPress, Macintosh
PAPER STOCK > Mead Signature dull, Gilbert Oxford

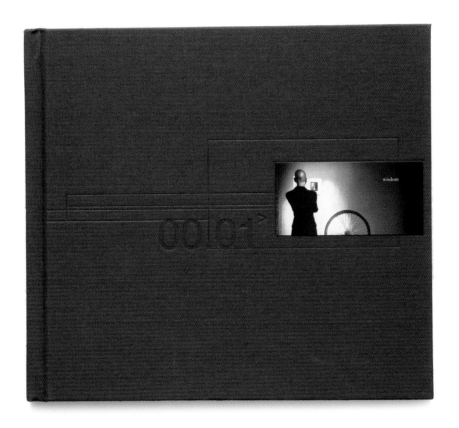

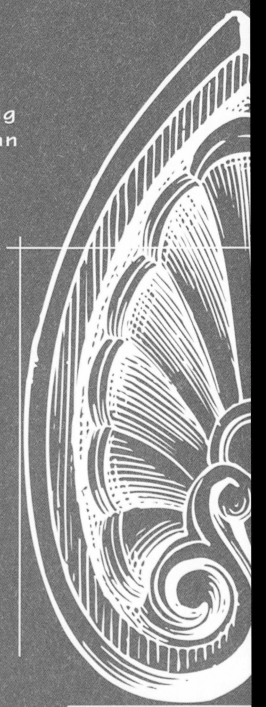

CHANGE ORDERS
Dr. Michael Cohen

Some Directors have
reported a decline in
enthusiasm from
members who are looking
for something more than
the same old thing.'
In a few cases, there
has been an overall
decline in attendance
and even drop-outs.
Dr. Cohen will draw
on his own
experience to
explore the likely
causes and offer
'change orders"
designed to
create a
rewarding, longer
lasting, and more
successful
study club
experience.

ARTS, ENTERTAINMENT +
EVENT **BROCHURES**

ヴィアッジョー空をめぐる旅
廣瀬智央

DESIGN FIRM › IT IS DESIGN Co.
ART DIRECTOR › Tomohior Itami
DESIGNER › Tomohior Itami
ILLUSTRATOR/PHOTOGRAPHER › Satoshi Hirose
CLIENT › TBS -J Britannica Co., Ltd.
TOOLS (SOFTWARE/PLATFORM) › Macos, Photoshop, Illustrator, QuarkXPress
PAPER STOCK/PRINTING PROCESS › Mr. B White

DESIGN FIRM › Hoffman Angelic Design
ART DIRECTOR › Andrea Hoffman
DESIGNER › Andrea Hoffman
ILLUSTRATOR › Ivan Angelic
CLIENT › The Seattle Study Club
TOOLS (SOFTWARE/PLATFORM) › Macintosh, Illustrator 8.0

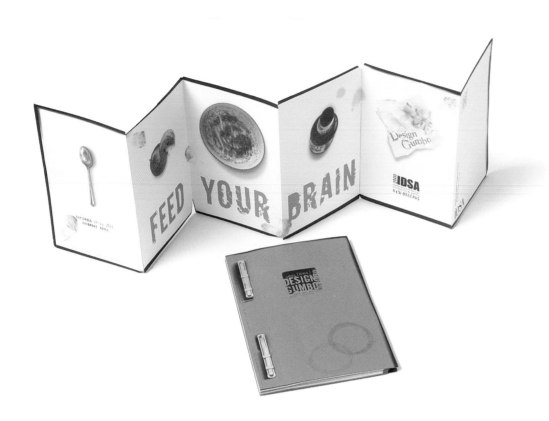

DESIGN FIRM › Bolt
ART DIRECTORS › Jamey Boiter, Mark Thwaites, Deanna Mancuso
DESIGNERS › Jamey Boiter, Mark Thwaites, Deanna Mancuso
ILLUSTRATOR/PHOTOGRAPHER › Stephanie Chesson
COPYWRITERS › IDSA & Bolt
CLIENT › IDSA
TOOLS (SOFTWARE/PLATFORM) › Photoshop, Illustrator, QuarkXPress
PRINTING PROCESS › 4-color, spot metallic

DESIGN FIRM › Future Brand, London

ART DIRECTOR › Wladimir Marnich

DESIGNER › Wladimir Marnich

ILLUSTRATOR/PHOTOGRAPHER › Magnum Photos

COPYWRITERS › L. Hertwig, R. Gautron, E. Steiner

CLIENT › Council of Europe

TOOLS (SOFTWARE/PLATFORM) › QuarkXPress

PAPER STOCK › Coated, silk finish

PRINTING PROCESS › Offset

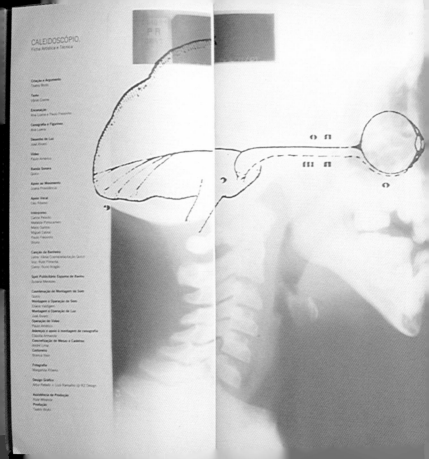

CALEIDOSCÓPIO.
Ficha Artística e Técnica

Criação e Argumento
Teatro Bruto

Texto
Vânia Cosme

Encenação
Ana Luena e Paulo Freixinho

Cenografia e Figurinos
Ana Luena

Desenho de Luz
José Álvaro

Vídeo
Paulo Américo

Banda Sonora
Quico

Apoio ao Movimento
Joana Providência

Apoio Vocal
Céu Álvarez

Intérpretes
Carlos Feliciano
Mafalda Portocarrero
Mário Santos
Miguel Cabral
Paulo Freixinho
Bruno

Canção da Banheira
Letra: Vânia Cosme/adaptação Quico
Voz: Rute Pimenta
Canto: Nuno Aragão

Spot Publicitário Espuma de Banho
Susana Menezes

Coordenação de Montagem de Som
Quico

Montagem e Operação de Som
Diana Vasligaro

Montagem e Operação de Luz
José Álvaro

Operação de Vídeo
Paulo Américo

Adereços e apoio à montagem de cenografia
Cláudia Armande

Concretização de Mesas e Cadeiras
André Lima

Costumeira
Branca Vale

Fotografia
Margarita Ktawa

Design Gráfico
Artur Rebelo + Lizá Ramalho @ R2 Design

Assistência de Produção
Rute Miranda

Produção
Teatro Bruto

DESIGN FIRM > R2 Design
ART DIRECTORS > Lizá Defossez Ramalho, Artur Rebelo
DESIGNER > Lizá Defossez Ramalho, Artur Rebelo
ILLUSTRATORS/PHOTOGRAPHERS > Lizá Defossez Ramalho, Margarida Ribeiro
CLIENT > Teatro Bruto
TOOLS (SOFTWARE/PLATFORM) > Freehand, Photoshop
PAPER STOCK > Munken lynx
PRINTING PROCESS > Offset

DESIGN FIRM ❯ Greteman Group
ART DIRECTORS ❯ Sonia Greteman, James Strange
DESIGNERS ❯ James Strange, Craig Tomson
COPYWRITERS ❯ Deanna Harms, David Kamerer
CLIENT ❯ Royal Caribbean
TOOLS (SOFTWARE/PLATFORM) ❯ Freehand, Photoshop
PAPER STOCK/PRINTING PROCESS ❯ Strathmore Elements smooth bright white

DESIGN FIRM > Trickett & Webb Ltd.
DESIGNERS > Lynn Trickett, Brian Webb, Katja Thielen
PHOTOGRAPHER > Adam Mitchinson
CLIENT > The London Institute
TOOLS (SOFTWARE/PLATFORM) > QuarkXPress
PAPER STOCK > Munken Lynx and Parilux
PRINTING PROCESS > Four-color lithography

The Hotel Patter and the Lamb's Players Theatre
Present

HOMETOWN
Christmas

A 1913 Celebration and Feast
Spring Valley, Bonita
Festival, Philip Patter
14 December 1913

The Menu

Hot Mulled Cider with Apples and Cloves
❋
Acorn Squash Soup
❋
Greens and Stilton
A Flavorful medley of broadleaf field farm, leaves,
and nuts, tossed with a vinaigrette dressing
❋
Roast Turkey Glazed with Farm Honey
Cornbread Dressing with Dried Fruit
Cranberry-Orange-Nut Relish
Sweet Potatoes and Chestnuts
Corn Stuffed Tomatoes
❋
Old Fashioned Lattice Top Apple Pie
Served with Ice Cream
❋
Coffee and Tea
Christmas Sugar Cookies

DESIGN FIRM > Sommese Design

ART DIRECTORS > Lanny Sommese, Pat Creyts

DESIGNERS > Lanny Sommese, Pat Creyts

ILLUSTRATOR/PHOTOGRAPHER > Lanny Sommese

COPYWRITER > Rick Bryant

CLIENT > Central Pennsylvania Festival of the Arts

TOOLS (SOFTWARE/PLATFORM) > Macintosh, Adobe Illustrator, QuarkXPress

PAPER STOCK > Beckett concept vellum

PRINTING PROCESS > Offset

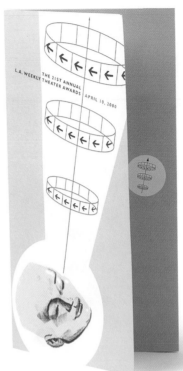

DESIGN FIRM > Dana Collins
ART DIRECTOR > Dana Collins
DESIGNER > Dana Collins
ILLUSTRATOR/PHOTOGRAPHER > Dana Collins
CLIENT > LA Weekly Theater Awards
TOOLS (SOFTWARE/PLATFORM) > Corel Draw, Photoshop, QuarkXPress

DESIGN FIRM > Inox Design, Milan
ART DIRECTORS > Alessandro Floridia, Mauro Pastore
DESIGNERS > Alessandro Floridia, Mauro Pastore
COPYWRITER > Elena Schiavi
CLIENT > MTV Networks
TOOLS (SOFTWARE/PLATFORM) > Freehand
PAPER STOCK/PRINTING PROCESS > Plexiglass, acetate,
four-color offset printing, one-color (white) serigraphic

DESIGN FIRM > IE Design
ART DIRECTOR > Marcie Carson
DESIGNER > Marcie Carson
ILLUSTRATOR/PHOTOGRAPHER > Nadine Froger
COPYWRITERS > Liese Gardner, Susan Cuadrado
CLIENT > Extraordinary Events
TOOLS (SOFTWARE/PLATFORM) > Macintosh, Illustrator, Photoshop, QuarkXPress
PRINTING PROCESS > Four-color, lenticular tip-in

DESIGN FIRM › Spatchurst Design Associates
ART DIRECTOR › John Spatchurst
ILLUSTRATOR/PHOTOGRAPHER › John Spatachurst
CLIENT › City Recital Hall, Angel Place
TOOLS (SOFTWARE/PLATFORM) › Illustrator, Photoshop, QuarkXPress, Macintosh Platform
PRINTING PROCESS › Offset

DESIGN FIRM > Oh Boy, A Design Company
ART DIRECTOR > David Salanitro
DESIGNERS > Ryan Mahar, David Salanitro, Ted Bluey
ILLUSTRATORS/PHOTOGRAPHERS > Ryan Mahar, Hunter Wimmer, Photonica, The Stock Market, FPG International
COPYWRITER > Carol Baxter
CLIENT > Mercury Interactive
PAPER STOCK > 50 lb. Lynx
PRINTING PROCESS > Offset, sheet fed

DESIGN FIRM › AXIS Communications
ART DIRECTOR › Craig Byers
DESIGNER › Tamara Dowd
ILLUSTRATOR/PHOTOGRAPHER › Various
COPYWRITER › S.I.T.E.S. (Smithsonian Institution Traveling Exhibition Service)
CLIENT › S.I.T.E.S. (Smithsonian Institution Traveling Exhibition Service)
TOOLS (SOFTWARE/PLATFORM) › QuarkXPress, Macintosh
PAPER STOCK › Donside Consort Royal, osprey, silk tint, 100 lb text and cover
PRINTING PROCESS › Four-color, plus two PMS and varnish

DESIGN FIRM > Lowercase, Inc.
ART DIRECTOR > Tim Bruce
DESIGNER > Tim Bruce
ILLUSTRATOR/PHOTOGRAPHER > Tim Bruce
CLIENT > Writers' Theatre Chicago
TOOLS (SOFTWARE/PLATFORM) > QuarkXPress, Macintosh
PAPER STOCK > Cougar

DESIGN FIRM › INOX Design, Milan
ART DIRECTORS › Claudio Gavazzi, Sabrina Elena
DESIGNERS › Claudio Gavazzi, Sabrina Elena
COPYWRITER › Michela Sartorio
CLIENT › MTV Networks
TOOLS (SOFTWARE/PLATFORM) › QuarkXPress, Photoshop
PAPER STOCK/PRINTING PROCESS › Opaque coated paper
PRINTING PROCESS › Four-color offset, gloss varnish

DESIGN FIRM > LA Weekly
ART DIRECTOR > Sheryl Scott
DESIGNER > Sheryl Scott
CLIENT > LA Weekly Music Awards
TOOLS (SOFTWARE/PLATFORM) > QuarkXPress, Photoshop

DIRECTORY OF DESIGN FIRMS

ADVERTISING INTERNATIONAL LIMITED
7 Bath Street, St. Helier
Jersey, C.I. JE24ST
United Kingdom
Tel: 01534 730001
Fax: 01534 735412
E-mail: adagent@ilt.net

AFTER HOURS CREATIVE
5444 E. Washington, Suite 3
Phoenix, Arizona 85034
Tel: 602-275-5200
Fax: 602-275-5700

ALTERNATIVES
875 6th Avenue, 26th Floor
New York, New York 10001
Tel: 212-239-0600
Fax: 212-239-1625
E-mail: julie@alternativesdesign.com

ARIAS ASSOCIATES
502 Waverley Street
Palo Alto, California 94301
Tel: 650-321-8138
Fax: 650-321-9250
E-mail: maral@ariasassociates.com

ARTICULATION GROUP/WILCO DESIGN
33 Bloor St. East, Suite 1205
Toronto, Ontario M4W 3T4
Canada
Tel: 416-922-7999
Fax: 416-922-1683
E-mail: joseph@articulationgroup.com

ASPEN INTERACTIVE
7036 Park Drive
New Port Richey, Florida 34652
Tel: 727-849-8166
E-mail: kweightman@aspenmg.com

AUSTIN DESIGN
161 Paradise Road
Swampscott, Massachusetts 01907
Tel: 781-593-4360
Fax: 781-593-5640
E-mail: wendyaustin@mindspring.com

AXIS COMMUNICATIONS
729 15th Street NW, Suite 900
Washington, DC 20005
Tel: 202-347-0060
Fax: 202-347-5331

BASE ART CO.
112 Oakland Park Ave.
Columbus, Ohio 43214
Tel: 614-268-3061
Fax: 614-268-3062
E-mail: base@ee.net

BBK STUDIO
5242 Plainfield Avenue NE
Grand Rapids, Michigan 49525
Tel: 616-447-1460
Fax: 616-447-1461
E-mail: yang@bbkstudio.com

BLOCH + COULTER DESIGN GROUP
2440 S. Sedelveda Blvd. #152
Los Angeles, California 90064
Tel: 310-445-6550
Fax: 310-445-6555
E-mail: victoria@blochcoulter.com

BOLT
1415 S. Church Street
Charlotte, North Carolina 28227
Tel: 704- 372-2658
Fax: 704-372-2655
E-mail: thwaites@mindspring.com

THE BONSEY DESIGN PARTNERSHIP PTE LTD
179 River Valley Road
05-01 River Valley Building
Singapore 179033
Tel: 65 339 0428
Fax: 65 339 0418
E-mail: postmaster@bonsey.com.sg

BURROWS
The Burrows Building
5 Rayleigh Road
Shenfield, Essex CM13 1AB
United Kingdom
Tel: 44 1277 246666
Fax: 44 1277 246777
E-mail: roy-hearne@burrows.impiric.com

CARBONE SMOLAN AGENCY
22 West 19th Street
New York, New York 10011
Tel: 212-807-0011
Fax: 212-807-0870
E-mail: leslie@carbonesmolan.com

CLARITY COVERDALE FURY
120 South 6th Street, Suite 1300
Minneapolis, Minnesota 55402
Tel: 612-359-4304
Fax: 612-359-4392
E-mail: treadwell@ccf-ideas.com

COUNTRY COMPANIES DESIGN SERVICES
1711 GE Road
Blooming, Illinois 61701
Tel: 309-821-2758
E-mail: tracy.sleeter@countrycompanies.com

COX DESIGN
5196 Hummingbird Road
Pleasanton, California 94566
Tel: 925-484-2711
E-mail: rcox@sjmercury.com

CREATIVE CONSPIRACY INC.
862 Main Ave., Suite 205
Durango, Colorado 81301
Tel: 970-247-2262
Fax: 970-247-1386
E-mail: nhannum@creativeconspiracy.com

CRITT + GRAHAM + ASSOCIATES
2970 Clairmont Road, Suite 850
Atlanta, Georgia 30329
Tel: 404-320-1737
Fax: 404-320-1920
E-mail: erin@crittgraham.com

CROSS COLOURS INK
8 Eastwood Road
Dunkeld West 2196 Johannesburg
South Africa
Tel: 27 11 442 2080
Fax: 27 11 442 2086
E-mail: cross@iafrica.com

DAMION HICKMAN DESIGN
22975 Caminito Olivia
Laguna Hills, California 92653
Tel: 949-261-2857
Fax: 949-261-5966
E-mail: DHD2YN@primenet.com

DAVID LEMLEY DESIGN
8 Boston Street, #11
Seattle, Washington 98109
Tel: 206-285-6900
Fax: 206-285-6906
E-mail: david@lemleydesign.com

DBD INTERNATIONAL, LTD.
406 Technology Drive West
Menomonie, Wisconsin 54751
Tel: 715-235-9040
Fax: 715-235-9323
E-mail: dbrier@dbdintl.com

DIDIER SACO DESIGN
10 Rue Des Jeuneurs
Paris 75002 France
Tel: 01 40 26 9696
Fax: 01 40 96 9596

DINNICK & HOWELLS
2943 Markham Street
Toronto, Ontario M6J 296
Canada
Tel: 416-921-5754
Fax: 416-921-0719
E-mail: jonathan@dinnickhowells.com

DOUGLAS JOSEPH PARTNERS
11999 San Vincente Blvd., Suite 201
Los Angeles, California 90049
Tel: 310-440-3100
Fax: 310-440-3103
E-mail: slambert@djpartners.com

EDELMAN PUBIC RELATIONS WORLDWIDE (ENKI)
636 Broadway, Suite 707
New York, New York 10012
Tel: 212-505-3543
Fax: 212-505-0846
E-mail: lana@enkiny.com

EMERY VINCENT DESIGN
80 Market Street
Southbank, Victoria 3006
Australia
Tel: 61 3 9699 3822
Fax: 61 3 9690 7371
E-mail: alison.orr@evd.com.au

ERBE DESIGN
1500 Oxley Street
South Pasadena, California 91030
Tel: 626-799-9892
Fax: 626-799-0906
E-mail: studio@erbedesign.com

FITCH
10350 Olentangy River Road
Worthington, Ohio 43085
Tel: 614-885-3453
Fax: 614-885-4289
E-mail: christina_cooney@fitch.com

FOCO MEDIA GMBH & CTE
Spitzwegstr 6
Munich 81373 Germany
Tel: 49 89 7463240
Fax: 49 89 74632424
E-mail: casar@focomedia.de

FORK UNSTABLE MEDIA GMBH
Juliusstrasse 25
Hamburg 22769 Germany
Tel: 49 40 432948 14
Fax: 49 40 432948 11
E-mail: svenja@fork.de

FOSSIL
2280 N. Greenville Avenue
Richardson, Texas 75082
Tel: 972-699-2125
Fax: 972-699-2071
E-mail: steven2@fossil.com

FUTURE BRAND, LONDON
Roger de Lluria 124
Parcelona 08037 Spain
Tel: 34 93 459 1477
Fax: 34 93 459 1816
E-mail: wmarnich@summa.es

GARDNER DESIGN
3204 E. Douglas Avenue
Wichita, Kansas 67208
Tel: 316-691-8808
Fax: 316-691-8818
E-mail: info@gardnerdesign.net

GEE + CHANG DESIGN
38 Bryant Street, Suite 100
San Francisco, California 94105
Tel: 415-543-1192
Fax: 415-543-6088
E-mail: earl@geechungdesign.com

GIORGIO DAVANZO DESIGN
32 Belmont Avenue E #506
Seattle, Washington 98102-6306
Tel: 206-328-5031
Fax: 206-324-3592
E-mail: info@davanzodesign.com

GIORGIO ROCCO COMMUNICATIONS
Via Domenichino 27
Milano 20149 Italy
Tel: 02461723/02461726
Fax: 02461728
E-mail: grcom@iol.it

GIOVANNI DESIGN ASSOCIATES
230 E. 44th Street
New York, New York 10017
Tel: 212-972-2145
E-mail: GDA70@earthlink.net

GOTHBERG + CO. DESIGN
Skarsgatan 66, Se-Y1269
Göteberg, Sweden
E-mail: design@gothberg.se

GRAIF DESIGN
165 E. Highway CC
Nixa, Missouri 65714
Tel: 417-725-1091
Fax: 417-725-6254
E-mail: matt@7coursedesign.com

GRANT DESIGN COLLABORATIVE
111 E. Marietta Street
Canton, Georgia 30114
Tel: 770-479-8280
Fax: 770-479-4384
E-mail: bill@grantcollaborative.com

GREGORY THOMAS ASSOCIATES
2812 Santa Monica Blvd., #201
Santa Monica, California 90404
Tel: 310-315-2192
Fax: 310-315-2194
E-mail: gregory@gtabrands.com

GRETEMAN GROUP
1425 E. Douglas, Suite 200
Wichita, Kansas 67211
Tel: 316-263-1004
Fax: 316-273-1060
E-mail: sgreteman@gretemangroup.com

GRIFFIN DESIGN
RR22, Box 6
1426 Butchers Lane
Blooming, Illinois 61701
Tel: 309-829-4295
E-mail: tracy@griffindesign.net

HAND MADE GROUP S. R. L.
via Sartori, 16
52017 Stia (Ar)
Italy
Tel: 39 0575 582083
Fax: 39 0575 582198
E-mail: handmade@dada.it

HOFFMAN ANGELIC DESIGN
317-1675 Martin Drive
Surrey, British Columbia V4A 6E2
Canada
Tel: 604-535-8551
Fax: 604-535-8551
E-mail: hoffman_angelic@telus.net

HOHENHORST ADVERTISING AGENCY
Never Kamp 30
Hamburg 20357 Germany
Tel: 49 171 1772127
Fax: 49 40 43209163
E-mail: etthing@foumat-UU.com

HORNALL ANDERSON DESIGN WORKS, INC.
1008 Western Avenue, Suite 600
Seattle, Washington 98104
Tel: 206-467-5800
Fax: 206-467-6411
E-mail: info@hadw.com

HUDDLESTON MALONE DESIGN
56 Exchange Place
Salt Lake City, Utah 84111
Tel: 801-595-6080
Fax: 801-595-6841
E-mail: dmalone@hmd.com

IE DESIGN
1600 Rosecrans Avenue
Building 6B
Manhattan Beach, California 90266
Tel: 310-727-3500
E-mail: mail@iedesign.net

INOX DESIGN
Via Terraggio II
Milan, Italy
Tel: 0039 02 8057007
Fax: 0039 02 8056283
E-mail: info@inoxdesign.it

INTRAWARE, INC.
2000 Powell Street
Emeryville, California 94333
Tel: 925-253-6523
Fax: 510-597-4851
E-mail: r-di@intraware.com

IT IS DESIGN CO.
204 Patio Harajuku, 3-15-22
Jingumae, Tokyo 150-0001
Japan
Tel: 03 3408 5753
Fax: 03 3408 7773
E-mail: itis@so-net.ne.jp

JILL TANNENBAUM GRAPHIC DESIGN & ADV.
4701 Sangamore Road, Suite 2355
Bethesda, Maryland 20816
Tel: 301-229-1135
Fax: 301-320-6620
E-mail: jill@jtdesign.com

JOSE J. DIAS DA S. JUNIOR
R. Nilza Medeiros Martins 275/103
05628-010 Sao Paulo, Brazil
Tel: 5511 37422996
Fax: 5511 8813887
E-mail: jjjunior1@ig.com.br

JULIA TAM DESIGN
2216 Via La Brea
Palos Verdes, California 90274
Tel: 310-378-7583
Fax: 310-378-4589
E-mail: taandm888@earthlink.net

KESSELKRAMER
Lauriergracht 39
Amsterdam 1016 RG
Netherlands
Tel: 31 20 530 1060
Fax: 31 20 530 7067
E-mail: special-k@kesselskrammer.nl

KAN & LAU DESIGN CONSULTANTS
28/F Great Smart Tower
230 Wanchai Road
Hong Kong
Tel: 852 2574 8399
Fax: 852 2572 0199
E-mail: design@kanandlau.com

LA WEEKLY
6715 Sunset Boulevard
Los Angeles, California 90028
Tel: 323-993-3561
E-mail: bsmith@laweekly.com
E-mail: sscott@laweekly.com
E-mail: dcollins@laweekly.com

LEE REEDY CREATIVE
1542 Williams Street
Denver, Colorado 80218
Tel: 303-333-2936
Fax: 303-333-3046
E-mail: lreedy@leereedy.com

LIBBY PERSZYK KATHMAN
19 Garfield Place
Cincinnati, Ohio 45202
Tel: 513-241-6401
Fax: 513-241-0417
E-mail: krisha_folden@lpkdesign.com

LORENZ ADVERTISING
9320 Chesapeake Drive, #214
San Diego, California 92123
Tel: 858-268-0291
Fax: 858-268-1146
E-mail: arne@lorenzadvertising.com

LOUEY/RUBINO DESIGN GROUP INC.
2525 Main Street, Suite 204
Santa Monica, California 90405
Tel: 310-396-7724
Fax: 310-396-1686
E-mail: studio@loueyrubino.com

LOWERCASE, INC.
213 W. Institute Place, Suite 311
Chicago, Illinois 60610
Tel: 313-274-0652
Fax: 312-274-0659
E-mail: sdvorak@lowercaseinc.com

MAGMA
Bachstraße 43
76185 Karlsruhe
Germany
Tel: 49 721 929 1970
Fax: 49 721 929 1980
E-mail: magma@magma-ka.com

MCMONIGLE & ASSOCIATES
818 E. Foothill Blvd.
Monrovia, California 91016
Tel: 626-303-1090
Fax: 626-303-5431
E-mail: david@mcmonigle.com

MELISSA PASSEHL DESIGN
1275 Lincoln Avenue, Suite 7
San Jose, California 95125
Tel: 408-294-4422
Fax: 408-294-4104
E-mail: ideasmpd@ihot.com

MICHAEL COURTNEY DESIGN
121 East Boston
Seattle, Washington 98102
Tel: 206-329-8188
Fax: 206-325-8256
E-mail: karen@michaelcourtneydesign.com

MICHAEL PATRICK PARTNERS
532 Emerson Street
Palo Alto, California 94301
Tel: 650-327-3185
Fax: 650-327-3189
E-mail: connie@mppinc.com

MORLA DESIGN
463 Bryant Street
San Francisco, California 94107
Tel: 415-543-6548
Fax: 415-543-7214
E-mail: dan@morladesign.com

O & J DESIGN
10 West 19th Street, 6th Floor
New York, New York 10011
Tel: 212-242-1080
Fax: 212-242-1081
E-mail: box1@designcarrot.com

ODEN MARKETING AND DESIGN
22 N. Front Street, Suite 300
Memphis, Tennessee 38103
Tel: 901-578-8055
Fax: 901-578-1911
E-mail: ssimmons@oden.com

OH BOY, A DESIGN COMPANY
49 Geary Street, Suite 530
San Francisco, California 94108
Tel: 415-834-9063
Fax: 415-834-9396
E-mail dbound@ohboyco.com

141 SINGAPORE PTE LTD
100 Beach Road #32-10 Beach Road
Singapore 189702
Tel: 65 392 9141
Fax: 65 392 9208
E-mail: onefouronespg@onefourone.com.sg

PALMQUIST CREATIVE
P. O. Box 325
Bozeman, Montana 59771
Tel: 406-587-2244
E-mail: Kurt@palmquistcreative.com

PARSONS PROMOTION DESIGN
66 Fifth Avenue
New York, New York 10001
Tel: 212-229-8905
Fax: 212-229-5113
E-mail: kime@newschool.edu

PENSARE DESIGN GROUP, LTD
729 15th Street, NW, 2nd Floor
Washington, DC 20005
Tel: 202-638-7700
Fax: 202-347-8430
E-mail: pensare@saggio.com

PEPE GIMENO-PROYECTO GRAFICO
C/Cadiers, s.n. Pol. d'Oradors
Godella, Valencia E-46110
Spain
Tel: 34 96 390 40 74
Fax: 34 96 390 49 76
E-mail: gimeno@ctv.es

PETERSON & CO.
2200 N. Lamar, Suite 310
Dallas, Texas 75202
Tel: 214-954-0522
Fax: 214-954-1161
E-mail: kristi@peterson.com

PISARKIEWICZ MAZUR & CO INC.
1 Wall Street Court
New York, New York 10005
Tel: 212-668-8400
Fax: 212-668-1366
E-mail: info@designpm.com

R2 DESIGN
Prçt D
Nuno Àlvares Periera, 20 5º FQ
Matosinhos 4450-218
Portugal
Tel: 351 229 386 865
Fax: 351 229 389 482
E-mail: r2design@mail.telepac.pt

R & M ASSOCIATE GRAFICI
Castellammare Distabia
Italia
Tel: 081-8705053
Fax: 081-8728505
E-mail: info@rmassociati.com

RBMM
7007 Twin Hills, #200
Dallas, Texas 75231
Tel: 214-987-6529
Fax: 214-987-3662

REVOLUZION STUDIO FÜR DESIGN
Uhlandstrasse 4
Neuhausen ob Eck 78579
Germany
Tel: 0049 7467 1467
Fax: 0049 7467 91155
E-mail: info@revoLUZion.com

SACKETT DESIGN ASSOCIATES
2103 Scott Street
San Francisco, California 94115
Tel: 415-929-4800
Fax: 415-929-4819
E-mail: elisalindenmeyer@sackettdesign.com

SAGMEISTER INC.
222 West 14th Street
New York, New York 10011
Tel: 212-647-1789
Fax: 313-647-1788
E-mail: ssagmeiste@aol.com

SAMATAMASON
101 South First Street
Des Plaines, Illinois 60016
Tel: 847-428-8600
Fax: 847-428-6564
E-mail: susan@samatamason.com

SAYLES GRAPHIC DESIGN
3701 Beaver Avenue
Des Moines, Iowa 50310
Tel: 515-279-2922
Fax: 515-279-0212
E-mail: sayles@salyesdesign.com

SHAMLIAN ADVERTISING
10 E. Sprout Road
Springfield, Pennsylvania 19064
Tel: 610-338-0570
Fax: 610-338-0675
E-mail: bigopen@aol.com

SHIBLEY PETEET DESIGN
3232 McKinney Avenue, Suite 1200
Dallas, Texas 75202
Tel: 214-969-1050
Fax: 214-969-7585
E-mail: candle@spddallas.com

SOMMESE DESIGN
481 Glenn Road
State College, Pennsylvania 16803
Tel: 814-238-7484
Fax: 814-865-1158
E-mail: lxs14@psu.edu

STOLTZE DESIGN
49 Melcher Street
Boston, Massachusetts 02210
Tel: 617-350-7109
Fax: 617-482-1171
E-mail: john@stoltzedesign.com

SPATCHURST DESIGN ASSOCIATES
230 Crown Street
Darlinghurst, Sydney NSW 2010
Australia
Tel: 61 2 9360 6755
Fax: 61 2 9380 5974
E-mail: steven@spatchurst.com.au

SUMMA COMUNICACIO
Roger de Lluria 124
Barcelona 08037 Spain
Tel: 34 93 459 1477
Fax: 34 93 459 1816
E-mail: wmarnich@summa.es

TRACY DESIGN COMMUNICATIONS INC.
118 S.W. Boulevard
Kansas City, Missouri 64108
Tel: 816-421-0606
Fax: 816-421-0177
E-mail: jantracy@swbell.net

TRICKETT & WEBB LTD.
The Factory
84 Marchmont Street
London WCIN IAG England
United Kingdom
Tel: 020 7388 5832
Fax: 020 7387 4287

TYCOON GRAPHICS
402 Villa Gloria
2-13-7 Jingumae, Shibuya-ku
Tokyo 150-0001 Japan
Tel: 81 3 5411 5341
Fax: 81 3 5411 5342
E-mail: mail@tyg.co.jp

UNIVERSITY OF IOWA FOUNDATION
One West Park Road
Iowa City, Iowa 52244-4550
Tel: 319-335-3305
Fax: 319-335-3310
E-mail: teresa-black@uiowa.edu

WAGNER DESIGN
1018 Fuller Street
Ann Arbor, Michigan 48104
Tel: 734-998-7120

WITHERSPOON ADVERTISING
1000 West Weatherford
Fort Worth, Texas 76102
Tel: 817-339-1373
E-mail: acomtois@witherspoon.com

ZAPPATA DISENADORES S.C.
Lafayete 143 Apzunes 11590
Mexico City, Mexico
Tel: 52 03 4075
Fax: 52 03 5667
E-mail: zappata@prodigy.net.mx

INDEX